Using Portuguese

This is a guide to Portuguese usage for students who have already acquired the basics of the language and wish to extend their knowledge. It covers both the Brazilian and the European varieties of the language, and differentiates clearly between them. The book gives detailed explanations of grammatical structures and semantic fields and, unlike conventional grammars, it pays special attention to those areas of vocabulary and grammar which cause most difficulty for English speakers. It also contains a special chapter for students who are familiar with Spanish, highlighting key similarities and differences between the two languages. Careful consideration is given throughout to questions of style, register, and politeness which are essential to achieving an appropriate level of formality or informality in writing and speech. Clear, readable, and easy to consult via its index, this is an essential reference for learners seeking access to the finer nuances of the Portuguese language.

ANA SOFIA GANHO is Assistant Professor of Portuguese, Brazilian and Lusophone African Literature and Film at Emory University, Atlanta, and the director of the Portuguese Program she started. She is currently finishing revisions to a manuscript on Portuguese and Latin American Modernism(s) and working on a book on postcolonialism and cinema in the context of Brazil, Portugal, and Lusophone Africa.

TIMOTHY MCGOVERN is Assistant Professor of Nineteenth- and Twentieth-Century Spanish and Portuguese Literatures and Language Teaching Methodology at the University of California, Santa Barbara, where he is also director of the Spanish and Portuguese Language Programs. He has published widely on topics related to Portuguese, Spanish, and Catalan literatures.

D0488020

Companion titles to *Using Portuguese*

Using French (third edition)
A guide to contemporary usage
R. E. BATCHELOR AND M. H. OFFORD
(ISBN 0 521 64177 2 hardback)
(ISBN 0 521 64593 X paperback)

Using Spanish
A guide to contemporary usage
R. E. BATCHELOR AND C. J. POUNTAIN
(ISBN 0 521 42123 3 hardback)
(ISBN 0 521 26987 3 paperback)

Using German
A guide to contemporary usage
MARTIN DURRELL
(ISBN 0 521 42077 6 hardback)
(ISBN 0 521 31556 5 paperback)

Using Russian
A guide to contemporary usage
DEREK OFFORD
(ISBN 0 521 45130 2 hardback)
(ISBN 0 521 45760 2 paperback)

Using Japanese
A guide to contemporary usage
WILLIAM MCCLURE
(ISBN 0 521 64155 1 hardback)
(ISBN 0 521 64614 6 paperback)

Using Italian
A guide to contemporary usage
J. J. KINDER AND V. M. SAVINI
(ISBN 0 521 48556 8 paperback)

Using French Synonyms
R. E. BATCHELOR AND M. H. OFFORD
(ISBN 0 521 37277 1 hardback)
(ISBN 0 521 37878 8 paperback)

Using Spanish Synonyms
R. E. BATCHELOR
(ISBN 0 521 44160 9 hardback)
(ISBN 0 521 44694 5 paperback)

Using German Synonyms
MARTIN DURRELL
(ISBN 0 521 46552 4 hardback)
(ISBN 0 521 46954 6 paperback)

Using Italian Synonyms
HOWARD MOSS AND VANNA MOTTA
(ISBN 0 521 47506 6 hardback)
(ISBN 0 521 47573 2 paperback)

Using French Vocabulary
JEAN H. DUFFY
(ISBN 0 521 57040 9 hardback)
(ISBN 0 521 57851 5 paperback)

Using Spanish Vocabulary
R. E. BATCHELOR AND MIGUEL
A. SAN JOSÉ
(ISBN 0 521 81042 6 hardback)
(ISBN 0 521 00862 X paperback)

Using Italian Vocabulary
MARCEL DANESI
(ISBN 0 521 81882 6 hardback)
(ISBN 0 521 52425 3 paperback)

Further titles in preparation

Using Portuguese

A Guide to Contemporary Usage

ANA SOFIA GANHO

Emory University

TIMOTHY McGOVERN

University of California, Santa Barbara

CAMBRIDGE
UNIVERSITY PRESS

PUBLISHED BY THE PRESS SYNDICATE OF THE UNIVERSITY OF CAMBRIDGE
The Pitt Building, Trumpington Street, Cambridge, United Kingdom

CAMBRIDGE UNIVERSITY PRESS
The Edinburgh Building, Cambridge, CB2 2RU, UK
40 West 20th Street, New York, NY 10011–4211, USA
477 Williamstown Road, Port Melbourne, VIC 3207, Australia
Ruiz de Alarcón 13, 28014 Madrid, Spain
Dock House, The Waterfront, Cape Town 8001, South Africa

http://www.cambridge.org

First published 2004
Reprinted 2005

Printed in the United Kingdom at the University Press, Cambridge

Typeface Ehrhardt 10.5/12 pt.   *System* LATEX 2$_\varepsilon$ [TB]

A catalogue record for this book is available from the British Library

Library of Congress Cataloguing in Publication data
Ganho, Ana Sofia, 1968–
Using Portuguese: a guide to contemporary usage / Ana Sofia Ganho,
Timothy McGovern.
    p.   cm.
Includes bibliographical references and index.
ISBN 0 521 79663 6 (pb.)
1. Portuguese language – Usage.   I. McGovern, Timothy Michael.   II. Title.
PC5260.M34   2003
469.8′2421 – dc21   2003046035

ISBN 0 521 79663 6 paperback

Contents

Abbreviations

adj	adjective
Br	Brazilian Portuguese
col	colloquial
f	feminine form
inf	infinitive
intr	intransitive
m	masculine form
pl	plural
Pt	European Portuguese
reg	regional
sg	singular
tr	transitive

Acknowledgments

One of the main goals of this book was to provide diversity of material, geographically and nationally speaking, rather than to limit samples and explanations to the standard discourse of a single country where Portuguese is the official language. In order to achieve this, the authors' knowledge of the Portuguese spoken in Portugal and Brazil was enhanced and/or supplemented as often as possible with the experience of speakers from specific regions, or countries (in the case of Lusophone Africa). The end result, was, we hope, a considerably more inclusive and richer linguistic and cultural, albeit not exhaustive, scenario.

We wish to thank these colleagues and friends who assisted us with their infinite patience and humor, their guidance and regional linguistic expertise and at times, too, with their imagination in the writing of samples: Marilene Barros-Luís, Arthur Bell, Sílvia Oliveira, Ana Santos-Olmsted, Heather Prado, Maria Elisa and Luís Antônio Gonçalves.

Ana Sofia Ganho and Timothy McGovern

1 Introduction

Portuguese is currently the mother tongue of nearly 200 million speakers and the official language of eight countries: Angola, Brazil, Cape Verde, East Timor, Guinea Bissau, Mozambique, Portugal, and São Tomé and Príncipe. It is currently growing in number of speakers owing to population explosions in most of these countries. There are also many creole varieties of Portuguese when it combines with native African languages. There are many variants of Portuguese, both within and between its different nations, including differences from northern to southern Portugal and a variety of phonological and lexical differences found in Brazil. The Portuguese language is traditionally broken into two major types: European Portuguese, which is spoken in Portugal (and includes the variations spoken in the Azores and Madeira archipelagos) and Africa (albeit with some differences); and Brazilian Portuguese.

In both European and Brazilian Portuguese there are major subdivisions. In the Portuguese of Portugal, the standard dialect is that of Lisbon and/or Coimbra, while some of the major variations are spoken in the islands of the Azores and Madeira, and in Northern Portugal. In Africa, the variants of Portuguese are enriched in vocabulary through contact with the various indigenous African languages and they have acquired their own pronunciation and some special verbal inflections. African vocabulary (mostly Kimbundu) can also be found in Portuguese from both Portugal and Brazil, being more abundant in the latter. In Brazilian Portuguese, some of the most identifiable variants are those of Rio de Janeiro, the Northeast, São Paulo, and the southern region.

1.1 The Portuguese language today

Africa

Besides its role as official language, Portuguese has combined with indigenous languages as a Creole, especially in Cape Verde, Guinea

Bissau, and São Tomé and Principe. These Creole dialects became, in the twentieth century, not only spoken languages, but also languages used in both written literature and film. One reason that Portuguese usage has survived in Africa is that no African languages were taught at school; Portuguese was necessary to access administrative careers, and citizenship until 1961. Those wanting to go to college attended a university in Portugal where, ironically they often met other pro-independence students. Portuguese is also used as a lingua franca.

The United States are home to a large Cape Verdean community with its most visible poles in the New England states.

Brazil

Brazil is the country with the largest number of Portuguese speakers (approximately 160 million). Brazilian Portuguese, which has become increasingly independent of the other varieties, is characterized by a large number of words derived from indigenous South American languages such as Tupi, and also from indigenous African languages, mostly from the Bantu and Yoruba groups, brought by slaves from the west coast of Africa from the sixteenth to the nineteenth centuries. European and Brazilian versions of Portuguese underwent different changes owing to the different influences to which each were exposed. For example, whereas Portugal was more susceptible to French influence, the 'creolization' factor was much greater in Brazil than in Portugal after the seventeenth century. In more recent times, Brazilian Portuguese has incorporated a larger number of words from Spanish and English due to calquing than has occurred in Portugal.

In Brazil the major centers which demonstrate the different characteristics of Brazilian Portuguese are São Paulo, Rio de Janeiro, the South, and the North East. Brazilian Portuguese also contains words and idioms that reflect the many ethnicities that Brazil has welcomed through time, in particular since the turn of the nineteenth century. A lax language policy (or lack of means to enforce one had it existed consistently), a precarious educational system, and a highly stratified society since colonial times, all resulted in a great gap between written and oral language. Only from the 1920s was there a conscious effort, on the part of writers associated with the *Modernismo* project, to bridge that gap and to bring colloquial and real-life Brazilian Portuguese into the written text.

Portugal

Portugal, where the language originated, is home to about 10 million speakers, both on the mainland and on the island communities of Azores and Madeira. Portuguese communities in North America and other continents, as well as recent trends in the immigration to

Portugal of Eastern Europeans and Africans, also contribute to the growing diversity of Portuguese. Peninsular Portuguese is much more homogenous, at least with respect to vocabulary, than the Portuguese spoken in Brazil and Africa. In the nineteenth and twentieth centuries, Portuguese has borrowed a significant number of words from French and English. Portugal entered the European Community in 1986 and currently Portuguese is an official language of the European Community.

Other speakers

Portuguese dialects are also currently spoken in small Asian enclaves, such as Macau (China), Goa (India), and is the official language of East Timor for historical reasons. A Portuguese-based Creole language is also spoken in Casamança, Senegal.

1.2 Linguistic registers and regional variations

Explanation of registers

Spoken and written language can vary to a great degree depending on the situation, the goal of the discourse, the level of education of both speaker and addressee, and the medium in which the discourse occurs. Thus, an e-mail to a friend, a business letter, a political speech, and an argument in a bar all elicit greatly differing styles of language. The three basic registers, described below, are addressed in this book.

R1

Consists of informal, colloquial speech. This may include slang, idiomatic expressions and proverbs, and informal syntax (i.e. discourse which does not necessarily follow the formal rules of grammar). R1 is normally used in conversations between family and friends.

A subcategory is R1* which indicates vulgar or obscene expressions. Many of these are included in this book since they are very much a part of the contemporary usage which this text seeks to describe. They are included more for the user's comprehension than for usage, since the learner of a foreign language may often misjudge the situation in which a certain obscenity may be employed.

R2

Is the standard or "neutral" register, most commonly characterized as that used in news broadcasts, or in a classroom setting. It is characterized by its lack of colloquialisms and its adherence to the rules of "correct" grammar, as well as its avoidance of vulgarity.

R3

This is the most formal register, characterized by the use of highly specialized vocabulary, archaic forms, and little-used but highly formal expressions and vocabulary; in literature it often includes a large number of symbols or metaphors. It may be used in literature, in legal or medical discourse, academic presentations, specialized professional presentations, and formal letters.

It is rare to find any piece of spoken or written discourse that belongs solely to one of the registers, but the words and expressions used in this book are still marked, where necessary, to aid students in their selection when speaking and writing.

Passages illustrating register and local variety

Example of R1 (European Portuguese): At the train station of Santa Apolónia, in Lisbon

Cristina: Sílvia, vamos antes para aquele guichê, este não aceita multibanco.

Sílvia: Ah, pois é. Estou a ver, deve ser por isso que tem uma bicha maior.

(10 minutes go by)

Man at the
ticket counter: Boa-tarde.

Sílvia: Boa-tarde . . . Eram dois bilhetes de ida e volta pro Porto, no Pendular, o do meio-dia, 'fachavor'. Em primeira.

Man: Ora são . . . oitenta euros.

Sílvia: Xii . . . caramba, até o comboio subiu com o euro! . . .

(Rodrigo comes up behind them)

Rodrigo: Olha quem são elas! Então, vão passear?

Cristina: Hã?! Epá, que susto, Rodrigo!!

Sílvia: Olá, Rodrigo . . . então, estás bom?

Rodrigo: Sim, vou andando, e vocês? Há que tempos que não vos via! Agora não se telefona, é?

Sílvia: Epá, só ontem é que acabámos os exames. O que é que fazes por estes lados? . . . que pergunta parva, não deves ter vindo comprar sapatos . . . ou vens apanhar o comboio, ou buscar alguém, calculo? . . .

Rodrigo: Sim senhora, está esperta, a menina, os exames fizeram-lhe bem, hein Cristina?

Cristina: Pois, sabes, normalmente não dá uma pra caixa, coitadinha . . .

Sílvia: Olhem, vocês os dois, vão ver se eu estou na esquina . . .

Rodrigo: Pois . . . o raio do comboio está atrasado, que chatice, vim buscar o meu irmão . . . bolas, queria sair daqui antes da hora de ponta . . . E vocês?

Cristina: Viemos comprar bilhetes, vamos amanhã ao Porto, passar o São João, sabe-se lá se amanhã não estava tudo esgotado.

Rodrigo: Ah . . . o S. João . . . então o Santo António aqui não vos chega? . . . IIh, pronto, pronto, não faças essa cara, já sei que és do Pórto, Sílbia, carágo . . .

Cristina: És mesmo alfacinha, Rodrigo. Eu também sou daqui, mas convenhamos, o São João do Porto é outra coisa!

Rodrigo: Eu sei, pá . . . estava só a meter-me com vocês . . . mas não se esqueçam de tomar um cimbalino por mim, que aqui na capital não temos cá disso . . . E não me apareçam a cheirar a alho!

Sílvia: Épá, é por essas e por outras que os tripeiros têm fama de responder à bruta . . . tem juízo, homem . . . já devias saber que o Pórto é mesmo uma naçon, e também temos água canalizada pra tomar banho, vê lá tu . . .

Cristina: Deix'ó lá, não sabe o que perde . . . Olha, temos um bilhete a mais para a peça d'hoje à noite no D. Maria, tem tido boas críticas. Qués vir?

Rodrigo: Épa . . . adorava, mas a Guidinha, aquela minha colega de curso, convidou-me há uns tempos para ir lá jantar a casa. Mas obrigadinho.

Cristina: Ah, sim, a Guidinha, aquela que fala pelos cotovelos? . . . Desculpa lá . . . eu sei qu'i éla é uma simpatia de pessoa.

Rodrigo: Fica pra próxima.

[LOUDSPEAKER] *"Intercidades com origem em Coimbra-B, linha cinco."*

Rodrigo: Até que enfim, estava a ver que nunca mais chegava!

Sílvia: Bom, nós temos que nos despachar, por causa das obras na autoestrada há mais gente a vir por Alcântara, deve haver engarrafamento de meia-noite. Depois diz qualquer coisa quando o teu irmão se for embora, está bem?

Rodrigo: Olha, ali vem ele, já estou a vê-lo . . . Está bem. Divirtam-se!

Cristina: Aquele é que é o teu irmão? Hum . . . nunca me tinhas dito que era tão . . . elegante . . .

Sílvia: . . . tão giro . . .

Rodrigo: . . . e eu, não sou? Quem sai aos seus . . . Mas olhem lá, vocês não 'tavam cheias de pressa? . . .

Sílvia: Hã, pressa? . . . Ah, o trânsito . . . Não faz mal . . .

Cristina: Pois . . . não faz mal . . . vais apresentar-nos, não vais? . . . Será que ele gosta de teatro? . . .

Greetings, forms of address, and interjections

boa-tarde, "good afternoon."

xii . . . caramba, "Oh . . ., man!"

hã?! "Hum?, what?". Expression of surprise.

épá!, "man!". An expletive: does not have any real meaning and is not used in standard Portuguese; it can also be used as a filler. A common variation is "pá."

que chatice, "what a drag!", "damn!". Slang and/or colloquialism.

iih, pronto, pronto, "Oh, ok, ok." *Pronto* can also mean "there, there" as an expression of comfort or reassurance to someone who appears to be suffering.

pois, "right." Expressing confirmation of what was just said. In a formal context, it can also mean "because" and introduces a subordinate clause.

até que enfim, "at last." In a slightly more formal context, it can be replaced by "finalmente" ("finally").

tchau, "bye," "see you." Portuguese spelling for "ciao"; used in an informal or colloquial context.

Idioms

à bruta	brusquely
de meia-noite	enormous
é outra coisa	it's something else
é por essas e por outras que	it's because of [comments like] those that . . .
fala pelos cotovelos	s/he's a chatterbox
lá	there
não sabe o que perde	doesn't know what [he] is missing
o raio de [o comboio]	the damn [train]
quem sai aos seus [não degenera]	I'm my father's son
têm fama de	are reputed to be
vai ver se eu estou na esquina	leave me alone! (lit. "go see if I'm around the corner")

Vocabulary

The subject matter of this dialogue relates to various specific contexts, and this is reflected in the vocabulary used by the three characters.

Means of transportation and related problems (train, car, traffic)

Alcântara	area of Lisbon, one of the main points of access to the city
autoestrada	highway, motorway
bilhetes de ida e volta	return tickets
cheias de pressa	in a hurry
Coimbra-B	name of the main train station in Coimbra
comboio	train
em primeira	in first [class]
engarrafamento	traffic jam
esgotado	sold out
hora de ponta	rush hour

Intercidades, Pendular	names of two types of inter-regional trains in Portugal
linha	track or platform number
obras	road works
Porto-Campanhã	name of the main train station in Oporto
Santa Apolónia	name of the main train station in Lisbon
trânsito	traffic

Transactions

guichê	ticket counter
multibanco	ATM, cash dispenser
bicha	line (another word for it is *fila* due to Brazilian influence, since *bicha* in Brazil is a pejorative term used to mean "homosexual")
um bilhete a mais	an extra ticket

Regional rivalry

o São João	popular festivities celebrating Saint John, for which Oporto is known
tripeiros	people of Oporto (tripe is a popular regional dish)
alfacinha	people from Lisbon
alho	garlic (people used to hit each other with garlic heads, gently, during this festivity)

Pronunciation and regionalisms

Pórto, the accent denotes an open sound as opposed to the semi-closed *o* as in *avô*.

Sílbia, in many northern regions of Portugal *v* is pronounced like *b*.

carágo,* "shit!". An interjection typical of Oporto; literally, it means "cock," here modified from *caralho*. Usually it would not need a written accent: this is used only to indicate the open quality of the vowel.

cimbálino, Oporto's word for espresso coffee; the term comes from the Italian espresso machine brand name. The graphic accent is added for pronunciation purposes.

Pórto é [mesmo] uma naçon, "Oporto is a nation in itself." Expression denoting the regional pride of Oporto people, who have traditionally seen themselves as the economic center of Portugal (it has certainly been a leading industrial center). In a thick Oporto accent, the final *–ão* tends to be pronounced *–on*.

deix'-ó lá, "come on, leave him alone." The direct object pronoun *o* [u] in "deixa-o" is contracted with the preceding, weaker vowel *a*.

d' hoje, "of today," "today's." The silent *e* in "de" is easily elided by the more open vowel *o*, [ɔ].

Qués vir, "Do you wanna come?" Syllables often get dropped in European Portuguese in colloquial contexts. It should read "Queres vir?".

qu'i éla, "that's her." The final, silent *e* in "que" acquires an *i* quality and becomes part of a diphthong with the semi-open vowel *e* (as in the verb form *é*) that follows.

pró, contraction of *para* and *o*.

Other vocabulary

elegante, smart, good-looking. Word more common to R2 and R3 discourse, here used as understatement because it refers to the brother of one of the speakers.

giro, cute, handsome. Word more appropriate in R1.

Syntax

agora não se telefona, "Now nobody calls [anyone else] anymore." The absence of a clear subject is intentional and ironic, since it is evident that he's accusing the two women of never calling.

apresentar-nos; estou a vê-lo. In European Portuguese the object pronouns are placed after the verb. In the second case, because the pronoun is a single vowel and the verb form ends in *–r* (*ver o*), for ease of pronunciation, changes are made to the spelling: the final *–r* is dropped, the *e* requires an accent to mark the stress, and an *l* is added in front of the *o*.

diz qualquer coisa, "give me a call," "stay in touch." Informal imperative followed by an indefinite form that here is meant to come over as less vague than it seems, a suggestion for further contact.

estava a ver que, "I was starting to think that . . . " This construction is used only in informal situations and is typical of European Portuguese; in Brazilian Portuguese the gerund is used instead.

estou a ver, "I see."

meter-me com vocês, "I was just teasing you."

não faz mal, "it's ok, no problem." The subject of the action referred to is usually understood.

não vos chega?, "isn't it enough for you?"

olha quem são elas, "look at them, it's . . . and . . .."

queria, "I'd like to." The imperfect of *querer* can be used to express intent in the past when there is still reasonable expectation that it will come to fruition, as opposed to the simple past or *pretérito perfeito* (= I wanted to).

sabe-se lá, "who knows if . . .?", "how can we know?"

será que ele . . .?, "I wonder if he . . ." The future, in an interrogative sentence, expresses the hypothetical.

só ontem é que acabámos os exames; o que **é que** fazes. Adding "é que" is typical of colloquial language and merely underscores the action described or alluded to.

vamos antes, "let's go rather."

vê lá tu, "can you imagine that . . ."

vou andando, "OK," "so so," "nothing new." Only used in colloquial, informal situations as a reply to a greeting; a common variation is the near-passive "vai-se andando."

Example of R1 (Brazil): At the mall

Carla:	Fernanda? 'Tá tudo jóia, menina?
Fernanda:	Oi Carla! 'Tá tudo legal, e você?
Carla:	'Tá tudo bem. E aí, seus pais 'tão bons?
Fernanda:	Sim, eles viajaram para Belo Horizonte, só por um final de semana.
Carla:	Ah, é? Por quê?
Fernanda:	Eles estão visitando minha irmã – ela 'tá tendo dificuldade no primeiro ano na UFMG.
Carla:	Ah, 'tadinha . . .
Fernanda:	Ela 'tá estudando, 'mais' estudando muito, mais que no vestibular, e não consegue tirar notas boas . . . e você, que 'tá fazendo aqui no shopping?
Carla:	Eu 'tou procurando um vestido pra festa do Guilherme. 'Cê 'tá indo, né?
Fernanda:	Não sei. . . . Realmente não tenho nenhuma razão nem vontade de sair, sabe?
Carla:	Deixa de sê' besta, menina! Vai ser bom pra caramba! A última festa que ele deu 'tava um espetáculo – 'tava bombando até as quatro da manhã!
Fernanda:	'Tá falando sério?
Carla:	Ué, claro! Foi bem legal. E 'cê sabe quem vai também, né?
Fernanda:	Quem?
Carla:	Marcelo!
Fernanda:	Nossa! É verdade? Ele é tão bonitinho, você não acha?
Carla:	Acho, e ele é super-bonzinho também!
Fernanda:	Então 'tá – eu vou!
Carla:	Isso! Bom – agora você tem que me ajudar a escolher um vestido pra hoje à noite.
Fernanda:	Eu gosto daquele preto ali – é super bacana!
Carla:	Não me faz gorda? 'Cê sabe . . . bumbum grande . . .
Fernanda:	Claro que não, menina! Vamo' entrar?

9

(In the store)

Store clerk: Pois não, em que posso ajudá-las?
Carla: Por favor, podia me mostrar aquele vestido na vitrine, no meu número?
Store clerk: Com certeza, acho que vai lhe ficar muito bem . . . a cabine é logo ali . . .
Carla: Obrigada . . . depois vem dar uma olhada, Fernanda . . .

(A few minutes later)

Store clerk: Então, gostou?
Carla: Gostei sim, vou levar . . . vou pagar com cartão de crédito . . .
Store clerk: Com certeza . . . deseja pagar em prestações?
Carla: Sim, pode ser . . .
Store clerk: Pode assinar . . . aqui?
Tudo certo . . . muito obrigada . . . Boa-tarde, volte sempre!
Carla, Fernanda: . . . obrigada, tchau!
Fernanda: Viu só, que vestido, vai ficar super elegante . . . Me pega mais logo e aí a gente compra uma torta de chocolate pra levar pra festa, 'tá?
Carla: 'Tá – boa idéia! Até logo.
Fernanda: 'Tá, tchau!

Interjections, forms of address, greetings, and pronunciation

ah, é?, "really?". Expression of incredulity, or interest in hearing more about what is being said.

ah, 'tadinha, "oh, poor thing." Abbreviated form of *coitadinha*, which is the diminutive form of *coitada/o*. For emphasis, it is sometimes followed by the preposition *de* and a pronoun (*de mim, de ti, de você, dele, de nós, de vocês, deles/delas*).

aí, "then." Although this adverb, which is sometimes used together with a demonstrative pronoun ("esse livro aí"), generally has a spatial meaning, in Brazil it can also refer to a moment in time, as in "at that time."

até logo, "see you later."

'cê, "you." Abbreviated form of *você*.

isso, "that's the way" or "there you go." Expression of approval or confirmation.

'mais,' "but," in this case. The words *mas* ("but") and *mais* ("more") can be virtually impossible to distinguish phonetically in Brazil, the only way of telling one from the other being the context in which they occur.

né?, contracted form of *não + é*; only occurs in interrogative sentences.

pois não, "hello." Form of politeness used by store clerks and generally anyone in the service sector. Although this greeting already contains the formula "May I help you?", another sentence making it explicit can follow for emphasis.

pra, "in order to." Abbreviated form of *para*.

se'. Abbreviated form of *ser*. The final *–r* in verbs is often considerably
  softened or even elided.

'tá, 'tão, shortened forms of *está* and *estão*, typical of colloquial speech.

tudo jóia /legal/bem, "everything's good/cool/well."

ué, "oh?!". Interjection expressing slight indignation or surprise, used
  in most parts of Brazil.

Vamo', "shall we go in?". It is very common for the final *–s* to be
  dropped in colloquial speech.

viu só, "did you see?"

Vocabulary and idioms

bacana	nice, cool
besta	silly, idiot
bom pra caramba/um espetáculo	very good
bombando	dancing, partying hard
bonitinho	cute, handsome
bumbum	butt, bum
cabine	dressing room
em prestações	lay-away payment mode, payment by installments
olhada	a quick look
super-bonzinho	very nice
torta	pie or cake
UFMG	Universidade Federal de Minas Gerais
vitrine	store window

Syntax

deixa de sê', "Stop being silly."

vai lhe ficar muito bem, "it's going to look very good on you."

[ter vontade] de sair, to feel like going out.

Example of R1 (state of Goiânia, Brazil): On the road

Marluí: Quantos mais quilómetros faltam pra chegarmos em Goiás?

Rossejane: Ah, não sei . . . não enche o saco, Marluí, você sabe quantas vezes já me perguntou isso? Devemos estar chegando perto . . .

Marluí: Uai . . . não sei, não tou contando, e você devia de saber, sim . . . não tá dirigindo? Tá na cara que não está prestando atenção, faz uma hora quase que matava a gente contra aquele muro . . .

Rossejane: O quê? Está casuando de mim? Não viu que eu me desviei pra mim não quebrar o carro naquele buraco no meio da estrada? Vê se não enche!

Marluí: E você, só sabe retrucar . . . que buraco coisa nenhuma. Só pode ser o sol quente na cabeça pra fazer você dizer abobrinha.

Rossejane:	Olha que te dou um tabefe!
Marluí:	Pra isso você ia ter que crescer mais um palmo.
Rossejane:	'Tá bom . . . beleza . . . não precisa falar mais na minha cabeça, estou de saco cheio das suas tolices . . . Me diz uma coisa, você 'tá cabulando hoje, sua cabeça-de-vento?
Marluí:	Ah, alguém tinha que vir contigo. Estou matando aula, sim, e você deveria estar agradecida de ter alguém para pedalar junto.
Rossejane:	'Tá bom, 'tá bom . . . Vamos deixar de conversa-fiada. Acho que faltam uns 45 km.
Marluí:	Já não aquento mais o calor e estou morrendo de fominha.
Rossejane:	Ah, Santo Deus, como é possível? Você acabou de comer uma melancia quando paramos.
Marluí:	Melancia não enche barriga . . .
Rossejane:	. . . e você enche um saco e tanto, hein!? Que matraca, ainda não se calou um minuto desde que partimos.
Marluí:	Pelo menos o tempo passa. Olha só, já estamos chegando. Vamos procurar pouso em uma pensão.

(*Some time later*)

Marluí:	Estou morrendo de cansaço e fome. A dona da pensão, cadê ela?
Senhor Raimundo:	Ela foi matejar mas volta logo.
Rossejane:	Psiiiiu, o que ele quis dizer com "matejar"?
Marluí:	Ela foi para o mato pegar lenha, sua anta.
Dona Espírito Santo:	'Tarde, moças em que posso lhe ajudar?
Rossejane e Marluí:	Queremos pouso e uma comida bem quentinha.
Dona Espírito Santo:	Pouso tem que sobra, mas comida já acabou. Eu servi a janta às 18:00 e até já fui cortar lenha pra amanhã.
Rossejane:	Mas não é possivel que não tem nem restodonte.
Marluí:	Que diacho é "restodonte"?
Dona Espírito Santo:	Riririri (*risos*) ela quis dizer "resto de ontem."
Rossejane:	Nossa . . . Nunca ouviu falar que é chique dizer "restodonte" ao invés de "comida amanhecida"?
Dona Espírito Santo:	Olha gente, eu posso esquentar um arroz e fazer um bife a cavalo.
Rossejane:	Não carece, não, Dona. A gente se vira . . .
Marluí:	Iii, que é isso, Rossejane, a Dona tá oferecendo! . . . Dona, vá e carca a espora nesse bife, estamos passadas de fome!

Interjections, forms of address, greetings, and pronunciation

[es]'tá, [es]'tou, "is" and "am." These are shortened forms of the Present of the verb *estar*, typical of colloquial speech.

ah, Santo Deus!, "Oh, Holy God!" Equivalent to "Minha Nossa Senhora" or its most common version, "Minha Nossa" or just "Nossa."

beleza, "ok," "cool." The rest of the sentence, "Everything is," is understood. This is not a form of address.

dona, "lady" or "madam." It can also be used as a form of addressing a woman, less formal than "senhora."

iii, que é isso, "Oh, come on."

olha só, "look." The Imperative points in the direction where something is to be found. The word *só* has no particular meaning in this context and is only used for emphasis.

olha, gente, "look here" or "listen, people." The Imperative can be used to draw attention to something that is about to be said.

psiiiiu, "pst!" Discreetly attracting someone else's attention.

sua anta, "you idiot" or "you silly." Refers to the tapir, a wild animal reputed to be dumb, but the speaker here is using it in an affectionate way. The possessive *sua* in Portuguese has the same function as the personal pronoun "you" in English.

tarde, "afternoon." Short, colloquial version of "boa-tarde."

uai, "huh?", "well . . ." or "what?". Interjection expressing slight indignation or surprise, used in some regions of Central Brazil, such as Goiânia and Minas Gerais.

Vocabulary and idioms

tá na cara (col)	it's obvious
casuando (reg)	making fun of
retrucar (reg)	to answer back
dizer abobrinha	to talk nonsense
buraco coisa nenhuma	no hole – (expressing incredulity: "my ass!", "my foot!")
tabefe	slap on the face
tolices	nonsense, silly
cabulando	the same as "matando aula"
matando aula	to miss class on purpose, to play/ be truant
cabeça-de-vento	air-headed, absent-minded
uma matraca (reg)	a chatterbox
conversa-fiada	idle, pointless conversation
cadê (col)	where is . . .?
dona da pensão	the hostel owner, landlady
a janta (col, popular)	the dinner
que diacho (reg)	what the heck, what the devil (*diacho* = *diabo*)
um bife a cavalo	a fried egg served on top of a beef steak
se vira	we'll manage
estamos passadas de fome (col)	we're way hungry, we're starving

Syntax

a gente, "we." Often used instead of the personal pronoun *nós*, especially in colloquial speech.

carca a espora, "spur on that horse." The expression attests to the importance of cattle and horses for daily chores in Central Brazil. It naturally suggests that a horse will move faster when motivated with spurs. In this metaphor, the speaker is replacing the horse with the beef steak to express the hope that it will get to her plate quickly. *Carcar* shows how the *l* has been replaced by the letter *r* in some words (originally, *calcar* = to press with one's foot or heel) in rural areas of Central Brazil.

devia de saber, incorrect use of the preposition *de*, something very common indicating very informal context.

ia, "would go." The imperfect is often used instead of the conditional in spoken language.

não carece, não, "it's not necessary." This archaism has survived in remote or rural areas. The repeated use of *não* at the end of a sentence is characteristic of spoken language.

não é possivel que não tem, "it's not possible that there aren't." This impersonal construction + *que*, in standard Portuguese, should be followed by the subjunctive, not the indicative.

não enche o saco, or only **não enche,** "will you quit . . .?" or "leave me alone!". Idiom based on the comparison of one's patience with a bag that gets progressively full. When one has hit the limit, one might say "estou de saco cheio," "I'm sick of it."

pedalar junto, "to accompany." The verb "to pedal" is used figuratively and it is understood that the speaker means "junto com você."

pra mim não quebrar o carro, "so that I wouldn't damage the car." Construction in which the prepositional pronoun *mim* is used instead of *eu*. This denotes both a regional background and an informal context.

pra, "to." This is the shortened form of the preposition *para*, typical of colloquial speech.

Example of R1/R2 (Creole from Cape Verde): from "Amor di Mundo," album *Café Atlântico*, Cesária Évora/Teofilo Chantre

In the table below, you will find some lines of a song in Cape Verdean Creole, then the Portuguese words from which the Creole might have derived (this is not a translation per se) and, finally, the rendering into English.

Creole	Portuguese words	English
Nh'amor é doce	*Minha amor é doce*	My love is sweet
Nh'amor é certo	*Minha amor é certo*	My love is certain
Nh'amor tá longe	*Minha amor está longe*	My love is distant
Nh'amor tá perto	*Minha amor está perto*	My love is close
El tá na mim	*Ele está em mim*	It is in me
Tcha'm cantá-bo nh'amor	*Deixa-me cantar para vós, minha amor*	Let me sing to you, my love
Ó mundo	*Ó mundo*	Oh world

Example of R1/R2 (Creole from Guinea-Bissau): "Bissau kila muda," from the soundtrack of *Udju Azul di Yonta*, by Super Mama Djombo

In the table below, you will find excerpts of a song in one of the three Creoles from Guinea Bissau, then the Portuguese words from which the Creole might have derived (and only those) and, finally, the translation into English. Please note that the Creoles from Guinea Bissau, depending on the region, have adopted words from European languages other than Portuguese, such as Spanish, French and English, although that is not evident in the text below. African languages from which the Creoles from Guinea Bissau have borrowed vocabulary, and sentence and word structure, include Mandinka and Bigajó; such borrowings are not translated in the Portuguese, but the Portuguese endings that have been tacked on are marked. The general meaning is then rendered into English. We have followed, for the most part, the translation in the CD liner.

Creole	Portuguese words	English
Nha camarada	*Minha camarada*	My comrade
Nha estimadu amigu	*Minha estimado amigo*	My dear friend
Nha djumbaidur	*Minha -or*	My confidant
Nha segredu	*Minha segredo*	My secret
Sinta bu nota	*Senta tu e nota*	Sit down and take notice
Kuma e ka na nota	*Como eles -nota*	How they do not take notice
Si e ká na nota	*Se eles -nota*	If they don't notice
Anos no na nota mamá	*-nós nota, mamã*	We do notice mother
E na nota tudu	*Eles nota tudo*	They notice everything
E findji kuma e ka na nota	*Eles finge que eles -nota*	They pretend they don't notice

(cont.)

Creole	Portuguese words	English
Bissau kila muda!	Bissau q'ela muda [Aquela Bissau muda]	How Bissau has changed!
Geba riu di nha tera	[Geba], rio da minha terra	Geba, river of my country
Kordon di prata di mamá Guiné	Cordão de prata da mamã Guiné	Silver necklace of mother Guinea
Ora ku bu na intchi	Hora que tu enche	When your waters come back
Bin ku kalma I susegadu	Vem com calma e sossego	Bring us calm and tranquility
Osprindadi di no povu mamá	Hospitalidade do nosso povo, mamã	The hospitality of our people, mother
E na nota tudu	Eles nota tudo	They notice everything
E findji kuma e ka na nota	Eles fingi que eles – nota	They pretend that they don't notice
Montanha nunka, nunka ka na muda	Montanha nunca, nunca –muda	The mountain never changes place
E carga panu	Eles carrega panos	They have brought fabrics
E fala mantenha	Eles fala [que Deus te] mantenha	They have said hello
E tchora e kansa	Eles chora e cansa	They have cried to exhaustion
Di si fidjus kombatentis	De seus filhos combatentes	For their fighting sons
E tchora alegria	Eles chora alegria	They cry of joy
No isa bandera	Nós iça bandeira	We have raised the flag
No tchora sperensa	Nós chora esperança	We have cried hope
No kansa tchora	Nós cansa chorar	We are tired of crying
N ka na tchora mas	– chora mais	I not going to cry anymore
E, n ka na torna	– torna	I am not going to start
Tchora mas	Chora mais	Crying again

Examples of R2: Newspaper articles

Journalistic discourse is characterized in Portuguese, as in English, by the use of impersonal speech in order to create an impression of objectivity on the part of the author. This is to let the events appear to narrate themselves, while the narrated facts are further legitimized in this case by the use of numbers and, finally, quoted speech from witnesses or experts. It is important to note also that written R2 often shares a large amount of vocabulary with R3 in

English. Acronyms are also common in journalistic writing, as in English.

Article from Brazilian daily paper *O Globo*

"Apostando no confronto," Soraya Aggege, SÃO PAULO

O Movimento dos Trabalhadores Rurais Sem Terra (MST) declarou guerra ontem em resposta à prisão de 16 líderes da organização que comandaram no fim de semana a invasão da fazenda dos filhos do presidente Fernando Henrique em Buritis, Minas Gerais. Líderes do MST ameaçaram com novas ocupações de propriedades e falaram até em fazer uma revolução para distribuir renda no Brasil. Ontem mesmo, às 6h30m, invadiram a Fazenda Santa Maria, administrada por Jovelino Carvalho Mineiro Filho, amigo do presidente e sócio de seus filhos na fazenda de Buritis.

Cerca de 150 sem-terra ocupavam a propriedade, no Pontal do Paranapanema, Extremo Oeste paulista, ontem à noite. As invasões no Pontal fazem parte de uma estratégia do MST de intensificar as ocupações em todo o país. Cerca de duas mil famílias já estão acampadas e com uma lista de 50 propriedades a serem invadidas na região.

– Estamos preparados para ocupar terras em todo o país. Agora é guerra. E já há muita gente pronta, já acampada, para tomarmos mais áreas – disse o líder do MST no Pontal, José Rainha Júnior.

Rainha disse que, para chamar a atenção e politizar a guerra, está disposto a invadir qualquer propriedade, até do senador José Serra, candidato do PSDB à Presidência.

– Rainha se acha impune, acima da lei. E quer fazer política com baderna. Com isso a população não concordará – reagiu Serra.

(*O Globo on-line*, http://oglobo.globo.com/pais/18380800.htm Rio, 26 de março, 2002)

Stylistic comments

The "neutral" register at work in this news article is characterized by its absence of colloquialisms and vulgarity as well as its adherence to the rules of "correct" grammar. However, the article reproduces a lot of direct speech, instead of reporting this speech in the third person, so its register may be in part R1.

Vocabulary

apostando, betting on, counting on a predictable outcome.
fazenda, large, ranch-like property with a house for the land owner; crops and/or cattle and horses.
trabalhadores rurais, peasants or rural workers. Their classification as "rural workers" bears the mark of the Marxist/socialist ideology prevalent in the MST.

17

Movimento dos Sem Terra, official organization of rural, landless, and often jobless workers and their families. They are generally forced to go from one large property to another in the interior and NE states of Brazil in search of rural work, which can be all but non-existent in times of draught. The goal that unites them is to push for land reform as the means to achieve a fairer land distribution. The Fernando Henrique Cardoso governments started a process of redistribution (*assentamento*) by buying small pieces of land and giving them to families. The process has been slow and is often hampered by fraudulent land titles and corrupt officials at the local level; by deliberate massacres incited by landowners; and by some unreasonable demands on the part of the MST. Finally, in an unlikely alliance, some landless workers have been known to get temporary jobs working for the ranch owners and lumber companies, cutting down trees, thus augmenting the size of the ranches and supplying cheap wood even from protected areas such as indigenous reserves.

invasão, ocupação, here, the act of "invading" or "occupying" a *fazenda*.

impune, acima da lei, someone above the law or who acts with impunity.

baderna (col), confusion, chaos.

Syntax

The following verbs/constructions are all typical of R2:

fazem parte de, are part of.
a serem [invadidas], to be [invaded].
concordará, future tense of *concordar*.
reagiu, reacted, responded.

Article from Portuguese weekly newspaper *O Expresso*

"Rebeldes testam novas pedagogias," Margarida Dias Cardoso

André deixou a escola aos 13 anos para ser trolha, mecânico, carpinteiro, «o que calhava». No seu currículo escolar, interrompido no 5° ano, somou três chumbos e incompatibilidades com professores e colegas. Mas três anos de vida activa entre adultos ajudaram-no a perceber que talvez fosse melhor ser estudante e, quando a assistente social lhe bateu à porta, aceitou sem hesitar a oportunidade de participar no PIEF (Programa Integrado de Educação e Formação).

«Já andava arrependido por ter deixado a escola e agora, que aqui estou, quero continuar», admitiu ao EXPRESSO André Marques, à procura, finalmente, de vencer as dificuldades de leitura e escrita para obter o certificado do 6° ano, juntamente com mais 15 colegas envolvidos nesta experiência educativa, em Santa Maria da Feira. Com idades entre os 13 e os 17 anos, estes jovens têm em comum o abandono escolar, o trabalho infantil e, em alguns casos, problemas de delinquência.

(. . .)

Num dos concelhos mais industriais do distrito de Aveiro, o PIEF surge no âmbito do Plano para a Eliminação da Exploração do Trabalho Infantil, um programa nacional que envolve os Ministérios do Trabalho e da Educação e contempla um conjunto de iniciativas em várias frentes, da formação profissional ao próprio ensino regular.

(*Expresso on-line*, Lisbon 3/23/2002)

http://semanal.expresso.pt/pais/artigos/interior.asp?edicao=1534&id_artigo=ES54096)

Stylistic comments

The "neutral" register at work in this news article is characterized by its absence of colloquialisms and vulgarity as well as its adherence to the rules of "correct" grammar. It is also visible in the choice of more learned vocabulary and passive voice constructions.

Vocabulary

rebeldes	rebels, troubled kids
testam (*testar*)	to try, to test
trolha	construction worker in charge of laying bricks, cement, etc.
mecânico	mechanic, probably working with cars or appliances
somou (*somar*)	to have, to count
chumbos	times somebody fails a course
colegas	classmates
abandono escolar	(R2/R3) dropping out of school
obter	to obtain, to get
experiência educativa	educational experiment
contempla (*contemplar*)	to contemplate, to consider
um conjunto [de]	a number [of]
várias frentes	different fronts (of action to deal with a problem)

Syntax

o que calhava, whatever one can find.

no seu currículo escolar, in his school life or career.

ajudaram-no, *ajudar* + *o*, to help him/it. The spelling change is meant to avoid possible confusion with "ajudaram-o," in which the final syllable would sound like "mo" (contraction of *me* + *o*).

lhe bateu à porta (*bater* "to knock"): "knocked on his/her door";
often used metaphorically.

andava, from *andar*: feeling a particular way or doing something.

arrependido por, feeling regrets about something. It can also be used
with the preposition *de*.

à procura de, looking for.

vencer as dificuldades, to overcome obstacles.

juntamente com mais, together with. "Mais" is not really necessary
here.

Com idades entre os [13] e os [17], with ages between . . . and . . .

no âmbito do, (R2/R3) integrated in or under the auspices of.

da [formação profissional] ao [próprio ensino regular], [ranging]
from . . . to . . .

Article from Mozambican on-line news service

**"Transformação de Armas em Enxadas: Moçambicanos
estendem TAE para Angola."**

O Projecto de Transformação de Armas em Enxadas (TAE) vai
colaborar na elaboração de estratégias visando a desactivação de
esconderijos e recolha de armas em Angola. Segundo Albino Forquilha,
coordenador da aludida iniciativa, já foram estabelecidos contactos
entre TAE, o Conselho Cristão de Moçambique e a organização
"Angola-2000", para troca de experiências no âmbito do processo de
consolidação e manutenção da paz.

Para Forquilha, a participação do TAE em Angola é o início do
processo da sua internacionalização. A proliferação de armas é um
problema comum para Moçambique, Angola, RD Congo e África do
Sul. Desde a criação do TAE foram recolhidas em Moçambique 260 mil
armas ou engenhos bélicos. Entretanto, estima-se que haja ainda mais de
10 milhões de armas fora do controlo do Estado. (*Notícias*, 10/08/02)

(August 9, 2002, http://www.mol.co.mz/noticias/2002/
0810.html#01)

Stylistic comments

The comments made on the language style of the articles from Brazil
and Portugal also apply here.

Vocabulary

enxadas	plows
estendem (*estender*)	to extend, in a metaphorical sense
elaboração	making or elaboraration
estratégias	strategies

esconderijos	from *esconder* "to hide"; places where something is stashed or hidden away
recolha	(re)collection
armas	firearms
manutenção	keeping, maintaining, enforcing
engenhos bélicos	war machines

Syntax

visando, gerund of *visar*: aiming at.
segundo, according to.
aludida iniciativa, aforementioned initiative.
já foram estabelecidos contactos, (passive voice) contacts have been made or established.
no âmbito do, (R2/R3) integrated in or under the auspices of.
problema comum para, a problem common to . . .
estima-se que, ("semi–passive" construction) it is estimated that.

Example of R3 (Brazil): A business letter

Ilmo. Sr.
Daniel Pirelli
Caixa Postal 8157
[postal code–"CEP"] São Paulo, SP

3 de outubro de 2000

Prezado Sr. Pirelli,

Dirijo-me a V. Sa. em resposta ao anúncio para a posição de diretor de marketing, conforme publicado na Folha de S. Paulo do passado dia 26 de setembro.

Estou terminando atualmente o MBA na área de marketing na USP. Anteriormente, concluí na PUC-Rio de Janeiro o bacharelato em gestão e administração de empresas, tendo também feito um estágio de seis meses na Coca-Cola, em Atlanta, nos Estados Unidos da América e, no Brasil, na Petrogás, departamento de vendas. Nessas companhias, desenvolvi campanhas promocionais para diferentes grupos etários e, na Coca-Cola, colaborei na pesquisa preliminar para lançamento de novas bebidas. Em anexo, lhe envio o meu curriculo vitae para maiores informações.

Acredito plenamente que minhas habilitações acadêmicas e experiência profissional, e meu conhecimento, em primeira mão, dos Estados Unidos e fluência em inglês me permitirão contribuir a um excelente desempenho na VitaSul.

Grato pela atenção de V. Sa., lhe apresento cordiais saudações.

Atenciosamente,
Luciano Johnson

Stylistic comments

Although the gap between spoken and written language in Brazil decreased significantly throughout the twentieth century, business letters contain some remnants of archaic formulas dating back to colonial times, especially in the forms of address. Other aspects of business-letter style worthy of notice are a preference for nouns where a subordinate clause would be used in spoken language, and for object pronouns and the future tense.

Abbreviations, and opening and closing formulae

atenciosamente, yours sincerely.

grato pela atenção de, literally "thankful for the attention given by [you]," i.e. "thank you for your time and consideration." The formality of the context justifies the use of the third person here.

Ilmo., abbreviation of "Ilustríssimo," "[your] most illustrious."

lhe apresento cordiais saudações, "I present my cordial salutations to you," i.e. please accept my best regards.

MBA, English acronym for Master in Business Administration.

para maiores informações, for further information.

Prezado, Dear [Sir].

PUC-Rio de Janeiro, Pontifícia Universidade Católica do Rio de Janeiro, private, Catholic university with campuses in various cities throughout Brazil; the name of the campus is usually given after the school's abbreviation and a dash.

USP, acronym for Universidade de São Paulo.

V. Sa., abbreviation of "Vossa Senhoria," "Your Highness" or "My Lord."

Syntax and vocabulary

anteriormente, atualmente, examples of adverbs frequently used in such letters; the *–mente* ending corresponds to the "–ly" ending in English.

C.E.P. (Código de Endereço Postal), zip/postal code.

conforme publicado, as it was published.

desempenho, performance.

fluência em inglês, "my fluency in English." In Portuguese, the use of the noun *fluência* makes the sentence sound more elegant and formal than simply saying "I am fluent in English."

grupos etários, higher register form for "age groups."

permitirão, "will enable [me]."

tendo também feito, "having also done." This formula, as in English, avoids the necessity of repeating the subject in what would be another "and I also did . . ." clause; the effect is a more economical and elegant style.

Example of R3 (Portugal): A business letter

José Carlos Leite
e Mª Manuela Fonseca Guedes
Digiforma Produções
Praça da República, n°12, 5° Dto.
[postal code] Porto

2 de Dezembro, 2001

Ex.mo Senhor
Dr. António Soares dos Reis
Presidente do Instituto Multimédia
Av. Infante Santo, n°128, 1°
[postal code-"código postal"] Lisboa

Ex.mo Sr. Presidente,

Vimos pela presente agradecer o subsídio de €50 000 que nos foi atribuído, via Digiforma Produções, com vista à realização do projecto "Multimédia e ensino secundário humanístico" para a concepção de actividades piloto a usar na sala de aula.

Tal como especificado nos documentos de candidatura, o projecto decorrerá entre Janeiro e Junho, estando a fase de avaliação prevista para o mês seguinte. Na medida em que o arranque do projecto se encontra dependente da aquisição de material técnico e equipamento, e dado o adiantado da data, agradecíamos que V. Ex.cia nos indicasse de que elementos necessita para efectuar o pagamento.

Gratos pela atenção dispensada, e com os nossos melhores cumprimentos,

José Carlos Leite e Mª Manuela Fonseca Guedes
Digiforma Produções

Stylistic comments

The gap between written and oral styles in European Portuguese is considerably smaller than in Brazil, the former leaving less scope for innovation and flexibility. However, business letters, even in Portugal, still use a number of formulae (opening, closing, place and date of writing) and rules considered important in order to make the desired impression which is, after all, the prelude to a successful transaction or to obtaining a job offer. As in the previous letter, there is a preference for nouns instead of subordinate clauses, and the future and the gerund occur frequently. Note also that sentences and clauses tend to be longer in Portuguese than in English, which is actually a sign of elegance as long as the message remains clear. On the other hand, formal, written Portuguese will avoid demonstratives such as "this" or "that," especially at the beginning of a sentence or clause, in favor of *tal*, except when the intended meaning is "the former" or "the latter."

Abbreviations, and opening and closing formulae

We have not repeated comments on expressions and abbreviations that also appear in previous letters, so please refer back to those.

5°, abbreviation of "quinto andar," fifth floor.

Av., "Avenida," "Avenue."

com os nossos melhores cumprimentos, literally "with our best regards," i.e. "Sincerely yours."

Dr., abbreviation of "Doutor," title used for anybody with a BA degree ("Licenciatura") in Portugal, in any subject except Engineering ("Eng.") and Architecture (no abbreviation).

Dto., abbreviation of "direito," door or apartment "on the right hand side."

Ex.mo, abbreviation of "Excelentíssimo," "[Your] most excellent sir."

gratos pela atenção dispensada: literally, "[we are grateful] for the attention [you have] given [to us]," i.e. "thank you for your time and consideration."

Mª, abbreviation of "Maria," given that this extremely common name is usually followed by a middle name.

n°, abbreviation of "número," [street] number.

V. Ex.cia, abbreviation of "Vossa Excelência," "Your highness" or "Your excellency."

Syntax and vocabulary

actividades piloto, model activities, pilot activities.

arranque, the official beginning.

com vista a, with the goal of, aiming to.

dado o adiantado da data, given how late it is [in the month].

decorrerá, will take place or occur; the use of the future can be justified by the formal context.

efectuar, to make; in a less formal context, "fazer" could be used instead.

estando, the same as "e está" which would be considered less elegant.

necessita, necessitate; in a less formal context "precisa" could be used instead.

pela presente, literally, "by means of the present letter," i.e. "we are writing to . . ."

Example of R3 (Portugal): a business letter, in reply to the previous one (would probably be on notepaper with letterhead)

Proj. 1377/2001
[sender's name and address if
letterhead is not being used]
Lisboa, 11 de Dezembro, 2001

Ex.mos Senhores
Drs. José Carlos Leite e Manuela Fonseca Guedes
Digiforma Produções
Pr. da República, n°12, 5° Dto.
[postal code-"código postal"] Porto

Ex.mos Senhores,

Com o objectivo de ultimar o processo de atribuição de subsídio a
Digiforma Produções, junto remetemos o documento em anexo, que
V. Exas deverão assinar e remeter ao Instituto Multimédia com a
possível urgência.

Queiram ainda V. Exas esclarecer qual o meio de pagamento
preferido, se um cheque emitido sobre o Banco Atlântico, ou uma
transferência bancária. Caso optem por este último método,
necessitaremos de um número de conta e do NIB correspondente.

Para quaisquer informações adicionais solicitamos-lhes que nos
contactem através do telefone (22) 274357.

Com os nossos melhores cumprimentos,

M.ª da Conceição Rodrigues
Chefe dos Serviços Financeiros

Stylistic comments

The comments made about the previous letters apply to this one as
well. One aspect worth mentioning here, however, is the use of
vocabulary specific to the context of a bank transaction.

Abbreviations, and opening and closing formulae

We have not repeated comments on expressions and abbreviations that
also appear in the previous letters, so please refer back to those.

Proj. 1377/2001, Project #1377 of the year 2001: system of indexing
references.
documento em anexo, "attached document."
junto remetemos, "we are enclosing."
para quaisquer informações adicionais, "Should you need any
further information."
Pr., abbreviation of "Praça," "Square."
V. Exas., plural form of "Vossas Excelências," "Your excellencies."

Syntax and vocabulary

caso, "in case"; in a less formal context, "se" or "no caso de" could be
used.

cheque emitido sobre, a check underwritten by [bank].

com a possível urgência, "with the possible urgency," i.e. "at your earliest convenience."

com o objectivo de, "with the goal of," i.e. "in order to."

deverão (*dever*), "will have to" i.e. "must." The future tense here is a sign of both the formal context and the urgency of the request.

necessitaremos de, "we shall need"; the use of the future can be justified by the formal context.

NIB, acronym for "número de identificação bancária," a number needed to make a wire transfer: routing number.

processo de atribuição de subsídio, "the process of attribution of the subsidy." In formal and written contexts in European Portuguese there is a marked preference for nominal sentence structures, instead of relative clauses and verbs, whenever possible. In English one might say: "[in order] to make available the subsidy that you have been granted."

optem, formal for "choose" or "decide."

queiram, "may you"; the Present Subjunctive is used here to make a polite request: "will you please."

remeter, to send or send back.

solicitamos-lhes, "we ask that you please"; in a less formal context "pedir" could be used.

transferência bancária, wire transfer.

ultimar, to finalize. In Portuguese, in a less formal context "concluir" could be used instead. This would be less formal than its English cognate "to conclude."

R3 registers

The comments below each text sample are solely intended to explain certain constructions and expand on the vocabulary used. They do not constitute suggestions as to how it should or could have been written otherwise.

Example of R3 (Portugal): Contemporary fiction, Agustina Bessa-Luís, *Um Cão que Sonha*, p. 79

Note on the author

Agustina Bessa-Luís is a writer from northern Portugal, residing in Oporto. Her prolific work contains a gallery of characters from the old world of rural mansions and property owners, generally a small circle where motivations range from pettiness to the instinctive defense of family patrimony, the latter usually undertaken by strong women. One could also devise a different category of works by this masterful writer, a category including research on historical characters such as Inês de Castro, in *Adivinhas de Pedro e Inês*. Nonetheless, one consistent characteristic stands out in all her works: the keen observation of human nature. If her characters are at times heroic it is not due to their virtues, because they have just as many faults as virtues; both together result in a dense web of human contradictions. Often the challenge which this writing presents is proportional to how easily the reader can follow and accept the author's maxims, which condense bits of wisdom about human nature. *Um Cão que Sonha* is said to be less dense in style.

"A favor da sua insignificância Léon tinha aquela tranquilidade que parece moderação e é uma ausência de paixões. Os pecados mortais nunca o interessaram o bastante para criar com eles situações. Nem compreendia como isso pudesse ser. Desejar a mulher do próximo, por exemplo, não tinha qualquer sentido porque essa mulher não existia mais. Andavam por toda a parte com aquela horrível audácia que elas tinham e que reclamava atenção como se a atenção fosse uma posta de peixe para grelhar. Com Léon, as coisas corriam bem e não chegavam a reclamar os seus direitos diante dele. Limitavam-se a olhar para ele com secura – a secura de que as mulheres são capazes quando não pressentem uma vítima, mesmo a amada vítima, sempre a mais distinguida entre todas."

Stylistic comments

In this extract the writer seems to prefer nouns and relative pronouns to clauses that would be closer in style to colloquial language (e.g. hypothetically, "Léon era um homem insignificante e ao mesmo tempo tranquilo. Parecia moderado, mas na verdade só porque não tinha paixões"). In this way, the emphasis is on the qualities themselves, not on the subject, and the writing acquires a sententious, maxim-like tone.

Syntax and vocabulary

as coisas corriam bem (*correr*), "things generally went well."
com secura, "in a dry manner."
como se a atenção fosse uma posta de peixe para grelhar, "as if attention were a slice of fish ready to go on the grill."
limitavam-se a (*limitar*), "they would simply/only . . ."
para criar com eles situações, here the standard word order has been changed for emphasis; otherwise, it would read "para criar situações com eles."

Example of R3 (Guinea Bissau): Contemporary prose, Abdulai Sila, *Mistida*

Note on the author

Many authors from Lusophone Africa, in addition to writing in Creole, also write in Portuguese, in a manner closer to the European variant and, in fact, often eloquently displaying old-fashioned or very formal constructions no longer frequently used in Portugal. Such authors include Germano Almeida (Cape Verde) and Abdulai Sila (Guinea Bissau). The text below, by the latter, is taken from his 1997 novel *Mistida*, a noun which seems to derive from the Maninka verb *misti*, "to want, wish, desire very intensely," plus the Romance suffix *da*.

"Era uma guerra que tinha começado algumas semanas antes. Sem nenhuma declaração formal, sem nenhum aviso prévio sem ultimato. E ainda por cima sem a sua presença. Foram apenas alguns dias de febre que a obrigaram a ausentar-se do beco onde passara quase uma vida inteira sentada e logo tinha sido desalojada. Quando voltou, o lixo já se tinha apossado do seu lugar. Pediu-lhe que se retirasse, mas foi ignorada e desprezada. Protestou um dia inteiro.

No dia seguinte, o lixo tinha crescido o dobro. Passou os dias a vigiar, uma semana inteira. Na escuridão da noite o monte ia crescendo, noite após noite, sem parar. Finalmente pediu socorro, não podia lutar sozinha contra forças tão poderosas e cruéis. Os reforços solicitados e mil vezes prometidos ficaram pelo caminho minado pelo egoísmo e pela pobreza de espírito. A solidariedade requerida perdeu-se nos confins do desespero."

(Abdulai Sila, *Mistida*, Bissau: KuSiMon, 1997)

(Excerpt taken from http://www.terravista.pt/ilhadomel/4201/paginas/abdulai_sila.htm)

Stylistic comments

In this novel, the striking element is style, understood as more than a knowledgeable choice and combination of vocabulary, or syntax. While the lines flow with grace and skillful ease, the narrative's strength resides in the use of images, situations, and characters: the somber atmosphere, a destitute old woman with a mysterious past, forever awaiting a change of regime; the town's trash which keeps growing mysteriously; the stereotypical, heartless dictator. If we are inclined to call these elements allegorical, Sila reminds us that there is nothing allegorical about them – they are the country's very reality.

Vocabulary

ausentar-se, to take leave or be absent. Another way of saying this, in a more colloquial register, would be "quando não estava lá."

aviso prévio, prior warning. Although the adjective is unnecessary, it is often used idiomatically with this noun, adding emphasis.

beco, small alley.

logo, no sooner, immediately after.

desalojada, thrown out, dislodged.

lixo, garbage, trash.

que se retirasse (*retirar*), (R2/R3) [I asked it] to withdraw.

desprezada, the object of scorn or spite.
o dobro, twice as much, double.
pediu socorro (*pedir*), asked for help.
solicitados, (R3) requested.
minado, mined.
requerida, (R3) requested.
confins, confines.
tinha começado (*começar*), it had started.
tinha-se apossado (*apossar*) "had taken possession, had taken over."
  A synonym would be "apoderar-se."

Syntax

e ainda por cima, "and on top of that." An expression less formal
  than many in this text, probably marking that the perspective is now
  the woman's, not the narrator's.
passara, (R3) "had spent"; slightly more formal or literary than the
  compound form "tinha passado." This form is now rarely used in
  spoken discourse.
ia crescendo, "was growing slowly but surely."

Example of R3 (Brazil): Contemporary fiction, João Ubaldo Ribeiro, *Viva o Povo Brasileiro*, p. 15

Note on the author

João Ubaldo Ribeiro long since earned the right to be controversial,
while being critical and funny at the same time. Like many other
contemporary Brazilian authors, he has a perfect command of
differing language registers, from the editorial or *crônica* to the new
historical novel, among others. The extract below contains a mix of
both those subcategories, as it chronicles cultural traits of the author's
fellow Brazilians while placing the action in the early colonial period.

"O comportamento das almas inopinadamente desencarnadas,
sobretudo quando muito jovens, é objeto de grande controvérsia e
mesmo de versões diametralmente contraditórias, resultando que, em
todo o assunto, não há um só ponto pacífico. Em Amoreiras, por
exemplo, afirma-se que a conjunção especial dos pontos cardeais, dos
equinócios, das linhas magnéticas, dos meridianos mentais, das
alfridárias mais potentes, dos polos esotéricos, das correntes
alquímico-filosofais, das atrações da lua e dos astros fixos errantes e de
mais centenas de forças arcanas—tudo isso, por lá, as almas dos mortos
se recusem a sair, continuando a trafegar livremente entre os vivos,
interferindo na vida de todo dia e às vezes fazendo um sem-número de
exigências."

Stylistic comments

Here the author is poking fun at one of the deeply rooted superstitions shared by many, that Brazil is the epicenter of a particular geomagnetic force. While the topic he chose could easily make it into a *crônica*, the register and tone used clearly show that this text is not one. Among the characteristics here is the abundance of adjectives qualifying the many nouns specific to the semantic field of mysticism and astrology, some of them possessing a root from learned Latin ("arcanas"). Moreover, the author relates this in the voice of a serious narrator chronicling scientific facts, but not without spicing up the tone a bit by making the phenomenon he is describing sound quite comical.

Vocabulary

alfridária, influence exerted by the planets, according to Arab astrologists.

arcanas, ancient. Term derived from learned Latin.

desencarnadas, [the souls] that have come out of the body.

diametralmente contraditórias, perfectly or absolutely contradictory.

é objeto de, is the object of.

inopinadamente, unexpectedly. This term is rarely used in spoken discourse.

pacífico, devoid of controversy.

potentes, powerful.

Syntax

alquímico-filosofais, "alquímicas e filosofais," "alchemical and philosophical." In the case of two adjectives closely related in meaning but supplementing each other, the first adjective is used in the masculine singular form whereas the second agrees in gender and number with the noun.

faz com que, "it has as a result." Not exclusive to R3.

resultando que, "from which it ensues that," "causing."

trafegar, to negotiate or do business.

Example of R3 (Mozambique): Contemporary fiction, Paulina Chiziane, *O Sétimo Juramento*, p. 29

Note on the author

Paulina Chiziane is part of the newer generation of Mozambican writers who grew up during the post-independence years, having experienced the internal struggles and external wars that often spilled over from countries like South Africa. She is also one of the first female writers to openly voice in her writing a critique of the society/societies, at once modern and traditional, that allow the repression of women. Even though other female writers, such as Lília Momplé, had denounced this and worked to correct it, the critique of repression comes across most powerfully and unabashedly in Chiziane's writing.

"Clemente recorda os mitos das aulas de história universal. Mitos de bestas e santos. De deuses e demónios. Mitos do amor à lua cheia. Mitos de dragões e papões. Foi o mito de Rómulo e Remo que criou Roma. Hércules. Zeus. Vénus. Foi o mito do nascimento de Shaka que criou o império Zulu. O mito da criação do mundo, segundo o Génesis, governa metade do planeta Terra e criou a superioridade do branco sobre o preto, do homem sobre a mulher. O mito de mpfukwa torna os ndaus temidos e destemidos. O mito da encarnação governa o universo dos bantus.
Vera volta ao quarto do Clemente vigiar o seu repouso. Encontra bisavó e bisneto em conversa fechada. Interfere."

Stylistic comments

In the excerpt, as in much of the author's writing, elements of African cultures and other mythologies co-exist with the modern world, its technologies and a post-colonial condition. The latter, or real, dimension is served by a terse and directly economical style, as in the last paragraph, made up of very short periods and expressive words.

Vocabulary

Most vocabulary in the excerpt relates to the mythologies of different cultures:

bantus, the Bantu are a very large ethnic (and language) group and can be subdivided into smaller less encompassing ones. One of the Bantu language groups most represented in Lusophone Africa is the Kimbundu.

branco, preto, words for colors, here designating groups of individuals with those phenotypes. These words are not capitalized in Portuguese even when they are used as nouns.

dragões, papões, dragons and bogeymen.

Génesis, spelled as in English except for the graphic accent.

Hércules, Zeus, Vénus, Greek deities. Their names are normally spelled identically in Portuguese and English, except for the graphic accents. "Zeus" is pronounced as a diphthong in Portuguese (as in the personal pronoun *eu*), unlike in English.

mpfukwa, hero of the Ndau people. The Ndau are part of the larger Bantu family and live in an area of inner Mozambique and Zimbabwe.

Rómulo, Remo, Romulus and Remus, the founders of the city of Rome.

Shaka, Chaka: Zulu warrior king who was feared by many other ethnic groups and the British colonial troops in South Africa.

temidos e destemidos, feared and fearless. This is a play on words, as they share the same root.

Example of R3/R1 (Angola): Contemporary fiction, Manuel Rui, "A Grade," *1 Morto & os Vivos*, p. 23

Note on the author

Manuel Rui Monteiro was born in Huamba in 1941 and his works combine social realism with biting irony and humor. Among the topics examined in his works, some of the most important include race and racial differences, social violence, and the use of symbolic characters. His concern with the social conditions of the working classes and the poor, combined with his erudite background (he completed his law degree in Coimbra), become obvious both in his use of common colloquial speech in his dialogues and in his highly ironic use of images.

"Primo Alfredo, custa-me mesmo e nem sei como dizer . . . devem estar chocas."

Salvador percebera. O parente se atravessara embora num esgar de estremeço na cabeça parecia soluço, no fim os olhos parados, a garganta engolida de contra vontade e foi por aí não obstante a estalar e bem espumada, inspiração dele, fundo, buracos do nariz maiores e pensar nos passados purgantes que as velhas costumavam obrigar só de uma vez. E antes de abrir outra, pegou na garrafa do primo, entornou três dedos no copo e provou. Devia ser assim a consideração e confiança, às vezes havia um azar e podiam pensar que foi veneno.

"Não é choca. Estão velhas. Vocês lá no Lubango também andam à rasca com cerveja?"

"Agora não. Já se vai vivendo."

"Pois aqui é isto e pra arranjar só no matanço." (. . .) "Nem dá para perceber. Todos os dias o primo se andar por aí vê caixas de cerveja de lata a andarem de um lado para o outro. Donde saem? Da puta que os pariu porque eu não as bebo. Quem as bebe? Eu não sou."

"Mas de algum modo elas saem, primo."

Salvador descascava agora jinguba, cabisbaixo, em flagrante desalento, quase vergonha. Não tinha nada para oferecer ao parente. E Alfredo não viera de mãos a abanar.

Syntax and vocabulary

a estalar e bem espumada, (R1) "[the beer rolled down his throat as if it were] clicking and foaming [like fresh beer]."

a garganta engolida de contra vontade, "his throat swallowed against his will." The syntax makes it sound as if it was the throat that was swallowed, as the object, not the agent, of the act of swallowing.

à rasca, in a tight spot or a difficult situation, here due to the scarcity of beer.

andarem de um lado para o outro, "circulating," "being transported back and forth, everywhere."

chocas [cervejas], flat, lacking carbonation.

consideração, [out of] courtesy or consideration.

custa-me mesmo, "it is really difficult for me."

da puta que os pariu, (R1*) "[out of] the whore that spit them into the world," i.e. from hell.

de mãos a abanar, literally "with his hands waving," i.e. empty-handed.

entornou três dedos no copo, "he poured some three-fingers worth into the glass" (i.e. approximately two inches).

esgar de estremeço, a facial expression denoting pain, here accompanied by a head "tremor."

inspiração dele, fundo, "[his] breathing in, deep."

jinguba, Kimbudu word for peanuts.

Lubango, city in Angolan province of Huíla, NE of Luanda.

não obstante, "nevertheless."

no matanço, "in the killing," i.e. exploiting the situation with the seller, illegally.

obrigar só de uma vez, "[they use it] to make us take it all in one gulp."

purgantes, purgatives/cleansing substances (for the digestive tract).

soluço, "hiccup."

viera, simple form of the pluperfect; alternatively "tinha vindo," had come.

Example of R3 (Portugal): Contemporary fiction, António Lobo Antunes, *Exortação aos Crocodilos*, p. 8

Note on the author

In António Lobo Antunes's many novels two thematic axes stand out, psychiatry and colonial Africa, and his writing reveals in great detail his first-hand knowledge of both fields. However, the mastery with which he represents the elusive thought processes of his characters, organizes the narrative, and examines topics central to Portuguese culture and history deserves far greater attention than his biography.

"a minha avó, em lugar de bater-me, mandou às empregadas que fechassem a porta, envolveu-me no cheiro de aguardente, esticou a orelha à direita e à esquerda, as galinhas e os salgueiros calaram-se, respeitosos, conforme o mundo se calava a uma ordem sua, cochichou

– Não contes a ninguém vou ensinar-te um segredo
sabia tudo, lia revistas em espanhol, conhecia as estrelas
Aldebarã
aconselhava testamentos e partos, despedia cozinheiras, adivinhava
os relâmpagos, jurava que na Galiza chove o tempo inteiro e nascem
rosas no mar, sempre vestida de branco como uma noiva antiga desde
que o meu avô morreu, exigia que lhe trouxessem as flores de laranjeira
numa redoma fosca, poisava a redoma no colo e ninguém se atrevia a
falar, as travessas deslizavam sem ruído, o meu tio doente dos pulmões
apagava a telefonia, o meu pai empoleirado na caixa registradora
ajeitava de imediato a gravata."

Stylistic comments

In a style reminiscent of the stream of consciousness, Lobo Antunes
skillfully maneuvers between characters' perspectives and their almost
involuntary memories. He sets his prose as free as he can from the
constraints of writing conventions: hence the sparse use of commas
and periods, and the ambiguity of marks of direct speech, in the
excerpt above. Another important trait in this excerpt is the poetic
tone conveyed by the use of certain images, such as the flowers'
evocation of innocence, and by the veiled suggestions that the
supernatural is at work (e.g. the grandmother's clairvoyance and the
roses in the sea).

Syntax and vocabulary

em lugar de, instead of.
envolveu-me, "she enveloped me."
esticou, "she stretched," i.e. listened attentively.
conforme, as, when.
cochichou, (R1) whispered.
Aldebarã, a star in the constellation Taurus; town in Galicia.
adivinhava os relâmpagos, "she guessed when lightning was
    coming."
noiva antiga: "a bride like in the old days."
flores de laranjeira: the orange tree flower, symbol of purity worn by
    brides.
redoma fosca: foggy, not completely transparent glass dome.
poisar, to put down [same as *pousar*].
colo, lap.
travessas, serving plates.
apagar, to turn off.
telefonia, the old name for a radio set.
empoleirado, sitting on, perched like a bird on a stick.
caixa registradora, cash register.
ajeitar, to straighten up.

2 Written expression

This section covers general rules for the written variant of the Portuguese language.

Note: a minor orthographic difference between European and Brazilian Portuguese is that the former writes a single *ç* where the latter would use a cç thus *infração/infracção*. This alternative spelling is rendered thus: *infra(c)ção*.

2.1 Accentuation

2.1.1 Diacritical marks

There are four diacritical marks in Portuguese from Portugal and five in Brazilian Portuguese.

1. The tilde (~) is used to indicate a nazalized vowel or group of vowels.

    Examples:
    João (John)
    corações (hearts)
    maçã (apple)

2. The circumflex accent (^) is used to indicate the pronunciation of a semi-closed *a*, *e*, *o*. This vowel is always stressed.

    Examples:
    português (Portuguese)
    avô (grandfather)
    Antônio (Br) (Anthony)
    ignorância (ignorance)

The circumflex is also used to indicate double vowels pronounced
   separately:
lêem (they read)
perdôo (I forgive)

In Brazil, the circumflex is also used in the following word:
vôo (I fly, the flight)

3. The "grave" accent (`) is used to indicate the contraction of the
    preposition *a* (to) with the feminine definite article *a* (the) or the
    following demonstrative adjectives and pronouns (that/those): *aquilo*,
    aquele, *aquela* and their plural forms.

    Examples:
    Vou à praia (I am going to the beach)
    Mostrei o apartamento àquele homem (I showed the apartment to that
       man)

4. The "agudo" accent (´) is used to indicate stress in the following cases:

    (a) Words ending in a consonant plus *a*, *e*, or *o* or in their plural forms,
        which are not stressed on the penultimate syllable.
    Examples:
    metáfora (metaphor)
    diérese (dierisis)
    avó (grandmother)

    (b) Words ending in *-m*, *-l*, or *-z* or their plural forms, when the last
        syllable is not stressed.
    Examples:
    álbum (album)
    alguém (somebody)
    fácil (easy)
    fáceis (easy, pl)
    mártir (martyr)

    (c) The plurals of words ending in stressed *–ol* and *–el*.
    Examples:
    papéis (papers)
    espanhóis (Spaniards)

    (d) To distinguish otherwise homograph words.
    Examples:
    saía/saia (I/he/she was leaving, or "Leave!" (command)/"skirt")
    país/pais (country/parents)

5. The dieresis (¨) is used only in Brazil to show that the letter *u* is
    pronounced after the consonants *q* and *g* and before the vowels *e* and *i*.

Although it is still in use, the spelling reform of 1994 agreed between Portugal and Brazil officially abolished the dieresis.

Examples:
agüentar (to tolerate)
freqüente (frequent)

2.1.2 Stress

The written accent in Portuguese is used to indicate either stress on, or the quality of, a vowel sound. In this section, stressed vowels are underlined. In Portuguese, each vowel is counted as one syllable and so are the diphthongs. The diphthongs in Portuguese are:

non-nasal: *ai, au, ei, iu, oi, eu, ui*
nasal: *ão, ãe, õe.*

Usually the pair *ou* represents a single sound, not a diphthong. It is pronounced like the *o* in [o] *avô.*

Any vowel with a written accent is the stressed vowel in that word.

Words ending in the vowels *–a, -e,* or *–o,* or these vowels followed by *–s, –m,* or *-ns,* are stressed on the penultimate syllable, unless they have a written accent. The stress for the vowels *a, e* and *o* is written with the circumflex accent (ˆ) if they precede –m or –n and sometimes –s.

Examples:
casa (house)
telefones (telephones)
escuro (dark)
caminham (they walk)
paisagens (landscapes)
agá (the letter H)
português (Portuguese)
café (coffee)
econômico (Br) (economical) [In this case a semi-closed *o* is pronounced]
económico (Pt) (economical) [In this case a semi-open *o* is pronounced]

Words ending in *–u, -i,* or these vowels combined with *–m, -s,* or *–ns,* or any other consonant, are stressed on the last syllable unless another vowel has a written accent.

Examples:
tatu (tattoo)
anis (anise)
comi (I ate)
rapaz (boy)
fácil (easy)
líder (leader)

Any vowel which is written with the tilde (~) is nasalized (as occurs in the pronunciation of *m* and *n* in English) and stressed.

Examples:

João (John)

corações (hearts)

anã (female midget)

All words stressed on a syllable preceding the penultimate syllable have a written accent.

Examples:

metáfora (metaphor)

fósforo (match)

Some monosyllables have a written accent to distinguish them from their homographs or homophones.

Examples:

por	(for)	pôr	(to put)
mau	(bad)	mão	(hand)
de	(of, from)	dê	(give) (formal command)
nos	(us)	nós	(we)

Some monosyllables are never written with graphic accents. Some examples are:

1. Definite and indefinite articles: *o / a / um / uma*, etc.

2. Clitic pronouns: *o, a*, etc.

   Example:
   O vi a semana passada (I saw him/it last week).

3. Relative pronouns: *que, qual, quais*, etc.

4. Conjunctions: *mas, nem*, etc.

5. Prepositions: *por, de, a, com, em*

6. Forms of address: *dom, frei, seu (senhor)*

7. The possessive pronouns: *meu, teu, seu*

8. Monosyllabic personal object pronouns: *mim, ti, nos*

9. The monosyllabic subject pronouns *tu* and *eu*

10. The Greek letter *phi*: *pi*

11. Nasalized monosyllables

    Examples:
    bem (well/good)
    bom (good)
    tem (he/she/it)

tom (tone)
som (sound)

The following monosyllables are always written with an accent:
cá (here)
lá (there)
má (bad [f])
mês (month)
pá (shovel)
pé (foot)
pó (dust)
quê (what)
sé (cathedral)
só (alone)
trás (behind)
três (three)
lã (wool)

Monosyllabic third-person plurals (many verbs have these) have a written accent:
dão (they [you pl] give)
põe (you put/he puts)
são (they [you pl] are)
têm (they [you pl] have)
vêm (they [you pl]come)

The following monosyllabic adverbs are written with a tilde:
não (not)
tão (as/so)

The plural forms of words ending in –aiz are accented.

Example: raízes

In the case of double vowels (-oo, -ee), the first is written with the circumflex accent if it is stressed.
Examples:
vôo (I fly) (Br)
lêem (they read)

Words in which the following vowels are pronounced separately (ai, au, ei, iu, oi, eu, ou) are also accented.
Examples:
saúde (health)
país (country)
reúnem (they gather)

Words ending in the following vowel combinations, which do not
form diphthongs (i.e. are pronounced as one syllable) have written
accents if they are not stressed on the penultimate syllable (*-ea*, *-eo*, *-ia*,
-ie, *-io*, *-ua*, *-ue*, *-uo*).

Examples:
ciência (science)
água (water)
Mário (Marius)

2.2 Punctuation

Portuguese punctuation is generally similar to English. Commas are
more frequent, especially in parenthetical expressions; semi-colons are
rarely used. Parentheses tend to be used instead of dashes. Unlike
Spanish, Portuguese does not use inverted question and exclamation
marks to introduce questions or exclamations. For examples of
punctuation the reader is referred to the text excerpts in the
Introduction.

2.3 Hyphenation

Hyphens are generally used to connect independent words into
compound words while at the same time preventing them from
becoming a single block. Hyphens are less frequently used in Brazil
than in Portugal. Below, you will find different groups of compound
words.

1. Compound words may be composed of a noun and an adjective, two
    nouns, or two adjectives, and may include a verbal form or a
    preposition:
    arco–íris (rainbow)
    cor-de-rosa (pink)
    chapéu-de-chuva (umbrella)
    latino–americano (Latin American)
    pára-choque (car bumper)
    nadador-salvador (lifeguard)
    fim-de-semana (weekend)
    bom–dia (good-morning)

2. Words formed with the following prefixes: *anti-*, *auto-*, *neo-*, *proto-*,
    pseudo-, *semi-*, *pan-*, *mal-*, *vice-*, *contra-*, *pre-*, *pós-*, among others.
    auto–retrato (self-portrait)
    pseudo-intelectual (pseudo-intellectual)
    semi-selvagem (semi-savage)

3. Words formed with the prepositions *sem, além, aquém, recém.*
além-mar (overseas)
aquém-fronteiras (within borders)
recém-nascido (newborn)

4. With the expression *haver de* (the periphrastic future). This hyphen is omitted in Brazil.
Hei-de viajar este Verão.
I will travel this summer.

Hão-de dizer a verdade.
They will tell the truth.

5. When the indirect and direct object and reflexive pronouns follow the verb.
Dá-me o livro.
Give me the book.

Eu vi-o.
I saw it/him.

Sentei-me.
I sat down.

6. The hyphen is also used to separate syllables at the end of a line of text, breaking before a consonant-vowel cluster: *ja-ne-la* (window). In the case of consonant clusters, if the cluster cannot begin a word, then it is separated: *cons-ti-tui-ção* (constitution).

   If a hyphenated word occurs at the end of a line of printed text, the hyphen is repeated at the beginning of the next line, as in this example containing the word "arco-íris":

   *Quando eu era criança, acreditava que a magia do **arco-***
   -íris se devia a uns pássaros da floresta,
   que traziam cada arco de sua cor quando parava de chover.

   When I was a child, I used to believe that the rainbow's magic was all due to little birds from the forest who'd each bring an arch of a different color when it stopped raining.

2.4 Capitalization

Capital letters in Portuguese are used as in English for personal names, names of places, holidays, abbreviations, and terms of address. Months and academic subjects are capitalized only in European and African Portuguese.

Biologia (Pt) (Biology)
Brasil (Brazil)
Janeiro (January)
Natal (Christmas)
Oceano Atlântico (Atlantic Ocean)
Senhor Gomes (Mister Gomes)

Capital letters are used in the titles of books and articles as in English.

Capital letters are not used in the following cases:

1. Days of the week: segunda-feira (Monday)
2. Nationalities: alemão (German)
3. Languages: português (Portuguese)
4. After a colon.

3 Vocabulary

3.1 Misleading vocabulary

3.1.1 False cognates

The following words are false cognates (often called false friends) because, while they closely resemble English words, their meanings are completely different or are used in different contexts.

Portuguese	English equivalent	English cognate	Portuguese equivalent
a(c)tualizar	to update	to actualize	realizar
a(c)tualmente	currently	actually	na verdade
advertir	to warn	to avert	impedir, evitar
agenda	planner	agenda	intenção baseada em convi(c)ções pessoais ou políticas
agonia	death pangs	agony	agonia, angústia
agonizar	to die	agonize	preocupar-se com
aplicar	to apply (pressure, method, knowledge, etc.)	to apply	concorrer
artífice	craftsman	artifice	estratagema
assistir	to attend an event, to watch (Br)	to assist	atender, ajudar
atender	to assist	to attend, go to	ir (à escola, espe(c)táculo, reunião, etc.)
barraca	shack	barracks	quartel
bordar	to embroider	to board to border	embarcar fazer fronteira com

coerente	consistent, congruent	coherent	bem organizado
colégio	private secondary school (Pt); high school (Br)	college	universidade
comando	military force; remote control	(to/a) command	mandar; ordem, elogio
compasso	(pair of) compass(es) (for drawing circles)	compass	bússula, compasso
compreensivo	understanding	comprehensive	muito abrangente, completo
concurso	contest	concourse	ponto de encontro
condu(c)tor (Pt)	driver	conductor	maquinista de comboio/trem
confidente	confidant	confident	confiante
consistente	thick (substance)	consistent	constante
conto	short story (contemporary)	account; a count (title of nobility)	conta; um conde
curso	degree, diploma	course (take a course)	matéria, aula (fazer uma aula)
dece(p)ção	disappointment	deception	engano
descendência	offspring	descent	ascendência
desgraça	(great) misfortune	disgrace	um evento que arruina moralmente a reputação de alguém
desmaio	fainting spell	dismay	profunda apreensão; desânimo
divertir	to entertain	to divert	desviar
editar	to publish	to edit	corrigir
educado	well-mannered	educated	instruído, cultivado
eficiente	efficient	efficient	eficiente (people); eficaz (things)
empregnar	to saturate	to get pregnant	engravidar
encontrar	to find, to come across somebody or something	to encounter	defrontar-se com (problemas)
esquisito	strange	exquisite	refinado
estar constipado	to have a cold (Pt)	to be constipated	ter prisão de ventre (Pt); estar constipado (Br)
eventualmente	in the event that, may be, possibly	(to happen) eventually	acabar por acontecer

êxito	success	exit	saída
fábrica	factory	fabric	tecido
formar-se	to graduate	to form	formar, fazer
hábil	skilled	able	capaz
ignorar	not to know	to ignore	não prestar atenção a ($\pm$ intencionalmente)
ingénuo	naïve	ingenious	engenhoso; de imaginação viva
injuriar	to insult	to injure	ferir, machucar (Br)
intoxicar	to poison	intoxicate	embebedar-(se)
introduzir	to insert	introduce	apresentar
largo	wide	large	grande
leitura	reading	lecture	apresentação, palestra
livraria	bookstore	library	biblioteca
longe	far	long	longo
mandato	political term; legal order; mission	mandate	ordem, missão; súmula dos desejos investidos num representante eleito
miséria	poverty	misery	tristeza
molestar	to bother; to mistreat (rare)	to molest	abusar sexualmente
novela	short story (especially in the nineteenth century)	novel	romance
obsequioso	generous with favors	obsequious	lambe-botas, untuoso
ordinário	vulgar	ordinary	vulgar; habitual
papel	sheet of paper; role, character (in play)	paper	papel; trabalho, apresentação (academic paper or presentation), document
parentes	relatives	parents	pais
porco	pig; dirty	pork	carne de porco
preservativo	condom (Pt)	preservative	conservante
pretender	to want to do or achieve	to pretend	fingir
prevenir	to warn	to prevent	evitar
processar	to process along; to bring a civil (law) suit (Pt)	to process	processar, dar andamento a
puxar	to pull	to push	empurrar

realizar	to make real; to do	to realize	dar-se conta
romance	novel	romance	situação amorosa; envolvimento amoroso
sensivel	sensitive	sensible	sensato
simpático	nice, friendly	sympathetic	compreensivo; solidário com uma causa/com alguém
tábua	plank	table	mesa
transpirar	to sweat	to transpire	ser descoberto, descobrir-se, vir a público

3.1.2   Homographs

Some Portuguese words have two different meanings depending on their gender.

	Feminine	**Masculine**
cabeça	head (of the body)	head (of an organization)
capital	capital city	money
corte	royal court	cut
cura	cure	priest
defesa	defense	fullback (football or soccer)
editorial	publishing house	editorial
final	final match	end
génese	origin	Book of Genesis
guarda	guard (the group), female guard	male guard
guia	document accompanying a person (e.g. a child) or a product to be transported; pass (allowing transport); a guide (book giving practical advice); female guide	male guide; touristic guidebook
moral	ethics; moral (of a story)	state of mind, spirits (high, low)
polícia	police force, a female officer (Pt)	a male officer

rádio	radio station	radius, radio set
recruta	recruitment in general, female recruit	male recruit
vogal	vowel	member (of a board or professional association/ organization [Pt])

Special homographs

The following words differ in spelling only in the use of written accent marks. Their meanings, however, are quite distinct.

copia	he/she/it/you copy(ies)	cópia	a copy
demos	we gave	dêmos	1st person plural subjunctive or imperative of *dar*
habito	I inhabit	hábito	habit
opera	he/she/it/you operate(s)	ópera	opera
nos	us; to us	nós	we
passeamos	we stroll/we strolled (Pt)	passeámos (Pt)	we strolled
pelo	por + the article *o*	pêlo	body hair
pode	he/she/it/you can	pôde	he/she/it/you could
por	for	pôr	to put
secretaria	a main office	secretária	secretary's desk, administrative assistant (f); secretária electrônica = answering machine (Br)
esta	this	está	he/she/it/you is (or "are")
para	to, for	pára	he/she/it/you stop(s)
vos (Pt)	to you (plural)	vós (Pt)	you (rural usage in Portugal)

The following words are pronounced slightly differently but are spelled exactly the same (i.e. none of them is written with a graphic accent). The use and pronunciation are dictated by context.

More open		More closed	
mo̲lho	I dip, a bunch	mo̲lho	sauce
e̲ste	East	e̲ste	this

3.1.3 Homophones

The following words are spelled differently but pronounced the same.

à	to the (preposition *a* + article *a*)	há	there is
acento	accent	assento	seat; I agree (from the verb *assentir*)
açular	to provoke (usually with animals)	assolar	assail (as in "the storm or bad weather is assailing Detroit")
asso	I roast	aço	steel
bucho	stomach (col)	buxo	bush
caçar	to hunt	cassar (Br)	to cancel (a license)
ceio	I eat supper	seio	breast; in the midst of
círio	candle	sírio	Syrian
concerto	concert	conserto	I repair, a repair
conselho	a piece of advice	concelho	an administrative division (like a municipality)
consular	consular	consolar	to console
coto	stub, stump	couto	refuge
cozer	to boil (cook by means of boiling water)	coser	to sew
elegível	eligible	ilegível	illegible
eminente	eminent	iminente	imminent
era	I/she/he/it was; an era	hera	ivy

graça	fun; grace	grassa	third person singular of *grassar* (to affect or assail)
nós	we	noz	walnut
passo	a step; I pass	paço	royal palace; official residence of an ecclesiastical or other dignitary
peão (Pt)	pedestrian; pawn (Pt)	pião (Pt)	toy top
roído	past participle of *roer* (to chew)	ruído	noise
sem	without	cem	one hundred
senso	sense	censo	census
sinto	I feel	cinto	belt
tenção	intention	tensão	tension
traz	he/she/it brings	trás	behind
viagem	trip	viajem	they/you (pl) travel (present subjunctive form)
voz	voice	vós	you (rural usage in Portugal)

Conjunctions and homophones

The following are pronounced the same but have different meanings and spellings depending on whether they are connected or separated.

contanto	as long as	com tanto	with so much
conquanto	even though	com quanto	with so much, with how much
acerca de	about	há cerca de	there are about (+ quantity)
porque	because	por que	why
senão	otherwise	se não	if not
contudo	however	com tudo	with all

3.1.4 Regional variations

Many words have different usages or meanings depending on the
geographical region or country of origin of the speaker. If the word is
used in Portugal but not Brazil, or vice versa, then there is no alternate
meaning given.

Portuguese word	English concept
academia (Br)	gym
autocarro (Pt)	bus
bica (Pt)	shot of espresso
bicha (Br)	homosexual (vulgar)
bicha (Pt)	line
bicho (Br)	term of endearment (col)
bicho (Pt)	animal
bilhete (Br) (Pt)	travel ticket
bilhete (Pt)	ticket for admittance
bonde (Br)	cablecar
cachorro (Br)	dog
cachorro (Pt)	puppy
cardápio (Br)	menu
carteira (Pt)	purse/wallet
carteira de identificação (Br)	card (as in identification card), work record
colar (Br)	to cheat in an exam
colar (Pt) (Br)	to glue together
comboio (Pt)	train
coroa (Br)	older adult with gray hair (col); spinster (col)
coroa (Pt) (Br)	crown
curtir (Br)	to enjoy oneself
curtir (Pt)	to tan leather; to make out (col)
eléctrico (Pt) (Br)	electric/electrical (adj)
eléctrico (Pt)	cablecar
ementa (Pt)	menu
ementa (Br)	list
fato (Pt) (Br)	fact
fato (Pt)	suit
geladeira (Br)	refrigerator
geleira (Pt)	ice chest; freezer
gelar (Br)	to freeze; to ignore
gelar (Pt, Br)	to freeze
ginásio (Br)	high school; indoor stadium
ginásio (Pt)	gym
gozar* (Br)	to have sexual pleasure

Portuguese word	English concept
gozar (Pt)	to make fun of, to have fun
grosso (Br)	rude
grosso (Pt) (Br)	thick
ingresso (Br)	ticket for admittance
ingresso (Pt) (Br)	college admission
malhar (Pt) (Br)	to forge metal
malhar (Br)	to work out (col)
moça (Br)	girl
moça (Pt)	girl (rural usage)
ônibus (Br)	bus
polaca (Br)	prostitute; person of very pale complexion
polaca (Pt)	Polish (f)
polonesa (Br)	Polish (f)
pomba! (Br)	interjection similar to "Darn!"
propina (Br)	small bribe
propina (Pt)	college fees
puto (Pt)	child
puxa! (Br)	interjection similar to "Wow!"
quadra (Br)	street block; tennis court
rapariga (Br)	prostitute
rapariga (Pt)	girl
sítio (Br)	small plot of land with a house
sítio (Pt)	particular location
trem (Br)	train
turma (Br)	a group of friends
turma (Pt) (Br)	class of students

3.2 Transitional phrases

Transitional phrases are necessary for the smooth movement between, and connection of, related ideas within a sentence, or paragraphs in written discourse, and are also highly useful in spoken discourse to fill the gaps between uttered ideas. These include many conjunctions, adverbial expressions, and prepositional phrases.

• **acho** (I think / I guess)

Deixei as chaves no meu escritório, acho.
I left the keys on my desk, I think.

• **apesar de** (in spite of the fact, although)

Apesar de não ter dinheiro, fui de férias.
In spite of the fact that I did not have money, I went on vacation.

- **assim** (in this manner / like this)

Se deve abordar o assunto assim.
The matter needs to be approached this way.

- **como é que hei-de dizer?** (how should I say/put it?) (Pt)

O meu vizinho é, como é que hei-de dizer, muito problemático.
My neighbor is, how should I put it, quite difficult.

- **de qualquer jeito / de qualquer maneira** (in any case)

Não sei se vou, ou não. De qualquer maneira, telefono-te.
I don't know if I will go or not. In any case, I will call you.

- **de jeito nenhum/de maneira nemhuma** (no way, under no circumstances)

De jeito nenhum! Não autorizo que os meus filhos passem toda a noite na discoteca.
No way! I won't let my children spend the whole night at a club.

- **digamos** (let's say) (Pt)

Encontramo-nos, digamos, às sete da noite.
We'll meet, let's say, at seven at night/in the evening.

- **embora** (even though)

Embora fizesse frio, fui à praia.
Even though it was cold, I went to the beach.

- **e depois** (then – meaning "directly following" / so what)

Corremos toda a tarde e depois tivemos de descansar.
We ran all afternoon and then we had to get some rest.

Não fui a trabalhar ontem, e depois?
I didn't go to work yesterday, so what?

- **em primeiro lugar** (first of all)

Em primeiro lugar, temos que fazer as reservas de avião, e depois pensaremos no hotel.
First of all, we need to make the plane reservations, then we will think about the hotel.

- **em resumo** (to sum it up)

Em resumo, *Romeu e Julieta* é a história de um amor trágico.
To sum it up, *Romeo and Juliet* is the story of a tragic love.

- **ena pá** (Pt) (an interjection like 'Wow!')

Ene pá, que golo! (col)
Wow, what a goal!

• **então** (then)

Se vocês não estáo bem aquí, então podem ir embora.
If you are not content here, then you can leave.

. . . e então, o que você acha dessa idéia? (Br)
So what do you think of this idea?

A organização de defesa do consumidor entrou en a(c)ção, e aí a indústria se mostrou mais cooperante.
The consumer protection organization stepped in, and then the industry showed itself more co–operative.

• **é que** (it is that / (to be) the one)

Você é que ficou encarregado de levar a Sílvia
You are the one who was supposed to pick up Silvia.

• **já que / posto que** (since)

Já que tu conhece Isabel, tu bem que podia me apresentar para ela. (Br) (col) (reg)
Since you know Isabel, you could introduce me to her.

• **mas** (but)

Quero ir ao concerto, mas não posso.
I want to go to the concert, but I can't.

• **na realidade / na verdade** (actually)

Não sou muito novo, na realidade tenho cinquenta anos.
I am not so young, actually I am fifty.

• **ou seja** (in other words)

O candidato conseguiu mais do que cinquenta por cento dos votos, ou seja ganhou com maioria absoluta.
The candidate won more than fifty per cent of the vote; in other words, he won (the election) by an absolute majority.

• **pá** (used to fill pauses in spoken discourse, similar to "huh" or "hmm" but also as an expletive like "man," "dude." It is not used in Brazil)

Estás bom, pá? (col)
How are you doing, dude?

• **pelo contrário** (on the contrary)

Não está claro. Pelo contrário, está bem confuso.
It isn't clear. On the contrary, it's quite confusing.

• **pois** (because)

O director não compareceu, pois houve qualquer mal-entendido.
The director didn't show up, because there was some misunderstanding.

- **pois é** (yeah/then / well / of course)

Pois é, ja sei que vais a Lisboa.
Yeah, I already know that you are going to Lisbon.

- **pode-se dizer** (one can say)

Pode-se dizer que as relações pessoais são mais fáceis no Brasil do que nos Estados Unidos.
One can say that personal relations are easier [to establish] in Brazil than in the USA.

- **por conseguinte** (therefore)

Eu sou brasileiro, por consequinte falo português.
I am Brazilian, therefore I speak Portuguese.

- **por exemplo** (for example)

Paulo viaja muito, por exemplo, a semana passada foi a Angola.
Paulo travels a lot, for example, last week he went to Angola.

- **por isso** (for that reason / that's why)

Jorge é muito mentiroso, por isso a gente não acredita nele.
Jorge is a terrible liar, that's why people don't believe him.

- **por último** (lastly)

Plane(j)amos a viagem e por último faremos as malas.
We'll plan the trip, and lastly, we will pack our bags.

- **por um lado . . . por outro lado** (on the one hand . . . on the other hand)

Por um lado, é importante estudar muito, por outro lado, também é preciso a gente se divertir.
On the one hand, it is important to study, on the other hand, it is also important to have fun.

- **quer dizer / isto é/ou seja** (in other words)

Os chefes de estado encontraram-se para discutir o desarmamento, o seja para discutir quem vai ter que desactivar os seus mísseis nucleares.
The heads of state met to discuss disarmament. In other words, to discuss who will need to deactivate their nuclear missiles.

Note: "i.e." is not used in Portuguese, since the letters coincide with the abbreviation for "isto é."

- **quer . . . quer** (whether or not)

Quer ela queira, quer não, vai ter de fazer isso.
Whether she wants to or not, she will have to do that.

• **vamos lá ver** (let's see) (Pt)

Vamos lá ver, quem pode ocupar-se de trazer as bebidas?
Let's see, who can take care of bringing the drinks?

3.3 Prepositions

3.3.1 *A*

Note: The preposition *a* joins in a contraction with the definite articles and the demonstrative adjectives and pronouns.

Vou às cinco.
I am leaving at five.

Fomos àquele cinema.
We went to that theatre.

3.3.1.1 Basic Meanings

(a) Destination, direction (generally corresponds to English "to")
Vou a Lisboa.
I am going to Lisbon.

(b) Point in time (clock time)
Daqui a um mês parto para São Paulo.
A month from now, I will leave for São Paulo.

(c) Location (meaning "at")
O homem estava ao seu lado.
The man was at her side.

(d) Upon
The idea of upon + gerund is expressed with *a* + *o* + infinitive
Ao chegar, viu que não tinha os documentos.
Upon arriving, he realized that he didn't have the documents.

3.3.1.2 *A* in time expressions

A corresponds to English "at," or "in," or "on" in many expressions relating to time

a 5 de setembro	on the fifth of September (in this case the "a" is optional)
à meia-noite	at midnight
a partir de	from a certain point onwards
a ponto de	on the verge of
a primeira vista	at first sight

a princípio	at the beginning
a tempo	on time, in time
ao almoço	at lunch
ao fim e ao cabo	in the end
ao longo de	along (spatial or temporal)
ao meio-dia	at noon
ao mesmo tempo	at the same time
aos poucos	little by little
às tantas da noite (Pt)	in the middle of the night
às vezes	at times
daqui a uma semana	a week from now
dia a dia	day by day
passo a passo	step by step
pouco a pouco	little by little

A expressing rate

a granel (Pt)	without any order/in large quantities
a oitenta à hora	at eighty kilometers per hour
a peso	by weight
à razão de	at the rate of
ao litro	by the liter
dois a zero	two–nil (for sports scores)

A expressing manner

à francesa, espanhola, etc.	in the style of the French, the Spanish etc.
a frio	after cooling down emotionally, without any warning
à imagem de	in the image of
à maneira de	in the style of
à minha maneira	my way
a pente fino	very thoroughly
a propósito	by the way, regarding
a sério	really; seriously
à toa	aimlessly
à tona	on the surface
à vista	in sight
à vontade	at ease
ao contrário	on the contrary
ao Deusdará	left to luck
às cegas	blindly

bacalhau à Braz	cod prepared according to the Braz recipe
comer à farta; comer à tripa forra (Pt)	to eat a great amount
de cabo a rabo	from one end to the other
de mal a pior	from bad to worse
fazer ao acaso	to guess, to do without thinking
passar a ferro	to iron
passar a limpo	to make a clean copy

A expressing position

à frente	ahead
ao lado	next to
à esquerda, à direita	on/ to the left/right
à porta	by the door
ao longe	far away
a luz de	in the light of
ao nível de	at the level of
ao pé de	close to
levar/ter ao colo	to hold close to the body
ao ar livre	in the open
ao alcance de	within reach of
ao fundo	in the back
à sombra	in the shade
ao sol	in the sun
ao telefone	on the telephone
ao ombro	over the shoulder
a meio	halfway
ao meio	in the middle
a bordo de	on board

Verbs which combine with *a*

aceder a	to give into; to access
acorrer a	to run to
acostumar-se a	to become accustomed to
amarrar a	to tie to
antepor-se a	to put (oneself) in front of
atrever-se a	to dare to
atribuir a	to attribute
brincar a	to play a role
brindar a	to toast
ceder a	to cede to, yield to
chegar a	to arrive in/at/on; to reach

chegar-se a	to move close to (a person)
cheirar a	to smell of
colar-se a	to cling to
começar a + inf	to begin
comprometer-se a	to promise to
concorrer a	to apply (to a school or for a job)
contribuir a (Br)	to contribute
dar (uma coisa) a	to give (something) to
decidir-se a	to decide to
equivaler a	to be the equivalent of
escrever a alguém	to write to someone
escusar-se a	to avoid
falar a	to speak to
faltar a	to miss (e.g. an appointment)
ficar a	to remain
incentivar/exortar/ incitar a	to incite to
ir a	to go to
ligar a	to pay attention to
limitar-se a	to limit oneself to
negar-se a	to refuse to
obedecer a	to obey
obrigar a	to oblige
orar a	to pray to
pertencer a	to belong to
presidir a	to preside over
reagir a	to react to
recorrer a	to resort to
reduzir a	to reduce to
referir-se a	to refer to
regressar a	to return to
remeter a	to send to
render-se a	to surrender to, to resign oneself to
renunciar a	to quit
resistir a	to resist
responder a	to respond to
restituir a	to give back to
saber a	to taste like
sair a	to take after
seguir-se a	to follow (only objects, ideas, concepts)
sobreviver a	to survive
tardar a	to take long to
temer a Deus	to fear God
tender a	to tend to
tornar a	to repeat
vir a	to come to

3.3.2 *Ante*

Ante is only used in a formal contexts to mean "in the face of" or "in the light of" or "faced with":

Ante as provas do crime ele confessou.
Faced with the evidence, he confessed.

Ante is also used in the expression *pé ante pé* which means "to walk on tiptoe":

O ladrão caminhou pé ante pé para não acordar ninguém.
The burglar walked on tiptoe in order not to awake anyone.

3.3.3 *Antes*

Antes means "before" and can be used alone and combined with *que* and *de* in order to express the following meanings:

antes	Alone, *antes* expresses "in a past time" or "before" **Antes, eu morava em Lisboa.** Before, I lived in Lisbon.
antes de	*Antes de* + a noun **Telefona-me antes do almoço.** Call me before lunch. *Antes de* + inf. **Não deves comer antes de nadar/** personal infinitive. (Pt) You should not eat before swimming.
antes que	*Antes que* + verb (always combines with subjunctive, but not with future subjunctive) **Antes que te esqueças, põe o frango no forno. (Pt)** Before you forget, put the chicken in the oven. **Chamei os bombeiros antes que o incêndio alastrasse.** I called the fire department before the fire spread.

3.3.4 *Após*

Após means after, and combines only with nouns and pronouns. *Após* is used mostly in formal speech and written language:

Examples:

Após as notícias, transmitiram uma sessão plenária do governo.
After the news, they broadcast a government plenary session.

Após alguns momentos de reflexão, o advogado falou para os jurados.
After a few moments of reflection, the lawyer spoke to the jurors.

3.3.5 *Até*

Até means "until," "up until," or "up to," and is used also with *que*.

até	*Até* combines with nouns and pronouns.
	Até ele me pedir desculpa, não vou falar com ele. I'm not talking to him until he apologizes to me.
	Não vou ao Brasil até ao Natal (Pt)/até o Natal (Br). I am not going to Brazil until Christmas.
	Portugal vai do Minho até ao Algarve. Portugal extends from the Minho region to the Algarve region.
até + personal infinitive	**Até vocês chegarem, vou estar aqui.** Until you arrive, I will wait here.
até que + verb	*Até* que combines with the subjunctive or the indicative.
	Até que você me dê as chaves, não posso usar o carro. I can't use the car until you give me the keys.
	Houve muitos terremotos até que o vulcão explodiu. There were many earthquakes up until the volcano exploded.

Expressions with *até*

Até amanhã. See you tomorrow.

Até já.	
See you in a bit / See you soon.	

Até logo.	
See you later.	

Até mais.	
See you.	

Até para a semana.	
See you next week.	

3.3.6 *Com*

Com means "with" and is used in a similar fashion as well as in a large number of expressions:

Examples:
Gosto de café com leite.
I like coffee with milk.

Fui com o meu filho ao circo.
I went with my son to the circus.

Expressions with *com*

com certeza
certainly

com pés e cabeça
understandable; well-organized

Com licença
Excuse me

Com os diabos (pronounced "C'os diabos")
Damn it!

Verbs which combine with *com*

acabar com	to finish with
apertar com	to put pressure on (someone)
arcar com	to bear
assustar-se com	to be frightened of
atordoar-se com	to be confused by
avistar-se com	to meet with
barafustar com	to argue with
berrar com	to shout at
carregar com	to carry (also figuratively "to bear with")
chatear-se com	to be annoyed with

combater	to combat
comover-se com	to be moved by (emotionally)
competir com	to compete with
conformar-se com	to conform to/with; to resign oneself to
contar com	to count on someone
cortar relações com	to cut off relations with
cruzar-se com	to bump into (somebody)
dar-se com	to socialize with, to be friendly with
decepcionar-se com	to be disappointed by
desculpar-se com	to excuse oneself for, to excuse oneself by
desgustar-se com	to be displeased by
discutir com	to argue with
distrair-se com	to be entertained by; to be distracted by
divertir-se com	to have fun by, to have fun with
drogar-se com (+ name of drug)	to use (drugs)
embirrar com (Pt)	to be annoyed with/by
empatar com	to tie with (as in a sports score)
encantar-se com	to be fascinated with
encontrar-se com	to meet with (somebody)
enervar-se com	to be upset by
entender-se com	to get along with
entreter-se com	to be entertained by
entusiasmar-se com	to become excited about
envaidecer-se com	to become vain about
espantar-se com	to be surprised by
fascinar-se com	to be fascinated by
fazer com que	to achieve through manipulation; to do everything in one's power to achieve (something)
fundir-se com	to merge with
gozar com	to make fun of
gritar com	to yell at
harmonizar-se com	to be appropriate for
haver-se com	to deal with (in a negative way)
horrorizar-se com	to be horrified at
impacientar-se com	to be impatient with/at
implicar com	to pick on
importar-se com	to be concerned with

importunar (-se) com	to bother (someone) with
indignar-se com	to become indignant because of
inquietar-se com	to become worried about
judiar com	to pester
ligar com	to match (as in clothing)
melindrar-se com	to get one's feelings hurt by
meter-se com	to tease
namorar com	to have an amorous relationship with
namoriscar com	to date
não poder com	to find unbearable
parecer-se com	to resemble (either physically or in character)
pegar-se com	to have an argument with
rabujar com	to be grumpy with
ralar-se com (Pt)	to worry about
reatar com	to reestablish a relationship with
refilar com	to complain in an annoying way
regalar-se com	to take great pleasure in something
resignar-se com	to be resigned to
rivalizar com	to be the rival of
simpatizar com	to like someone
solidarizar-se com	to share solidarity with
sonhar com	to dream of
transigir com	to tolerate
zangar-se com	to get mad at

3.3.7   Contra

Contra corresponds to "against," both physically and figuratively.

Examples:
Os revolucionários eram contra a ditadura.
The revolutionaries were against the dictatorship.

Puseram os móveis contra a parede para poder pôr o tapete novo no centro da sala.
They put the furniture against the wall in order to lay the new carpet in the middle of the living room floor.

A equipa do Brasil jogou contra a Argentina.
The Brazilian team played against Argentina.

O caso do estado contra Pinochet nunca se realizou.
The case of the State versus Pinochet never reached the courts.

3.3.8 *De*

Note: The preposition *de* joins in a contraction with the definite articles, the third person personal pronouns, and the demonstrative adjectives and pronouns.

Examples:
Meus pais estarão aqui a partir das cinco.
My parents will be here from 5 o'clock on.

Estes discos são dela.
These records are hers.

Daquele homem não podes esperar nada. (Pt)
You cannot expect anything from that man.

Basic uses

1. Movement from (in space and time)

    Examples:
    Eu voltei da capital ontem.
    I returned from the capital yesterday.

    Vou estar aqui das seis às oito.
    I will be here from six o'clock to eight.

2. Composition

    Example:
    Prefiro móveis de madeira a de metal.
    I prefer wooden furniture over metal.

3. Origin

    Example:
    Sou de Lisboa.
    I am from Lisbon.

4. Combined with *o que* in order to express "than" in comparisons

    Example:
    Sou mais responsável do que o meu irmão.
    I am more responsible than my brother.

5. Used with the superlative in order to express "in" or "on"

    Example:
    O pobre diabo julga-se o homem mais importante do mundo.
    The poor fool considers himself the most important man on
    earth.

6. Possession

   Example:
   Este livro é do Luís.
   This book is Luis's.

7. Price and measurement

   Examples:
   Uma nota de dez reais.
   A ten-real bill.

   Um selo de dois euros.
   A two-euro stamp.

   Um garrafão de cinco litros.
   A five-liter bottle/jug.

   A temperatura prevista para hoje é de 30°.
   The estimated high temperature today is 30°.

   A maratonista correu uma distância de quarenta quilómetros em menos de duas horas.
   The marathon runner ran a distance of forty kilometers in less than two hours.

8. Means of transportation

   Example:
   Nunca ando de avião, tenho medo.
   I never take the airplane, I'm afraid.

   Note: To indicate "by foot" or "on foot," the preposition "a" is used.

   Example:
   Eu ando a pé sempre que posso.
   I go on foot/walk whenever I can.

3.3.8.1 Expressions with *de*

aberto de par em par	wide open
atirar-se de cabeça	to jump in head first
cair (estar) de bruços	to fall on one's face
de cavalo para burro	from good to bad
de certa maneira/de certo modo	in a way
de cor e salteado	by heart (memorized)
de costas	from the back
de frente	facing
de graça	free (for no money)
de guarda	on guard
de lado	sideways

de longe	by a long shot
de luto	in mourning
de mal a pior	from bad to worse
de maneira nenhuma	no way
de memória	from memory, by heart
de novo	again
de ouvido	by ear
de passagem	just passing by, in passing
de presente	as a gift
de propósito	on purpose
de qualquer maneira	carelessly; in any case
de repente	suddenly
de sobra	extra
de um lado para o outro	from one side to the other
de um trago	in one gulp
de uma vez	at once, once and for all
de vez em quando	once in a while
estar de bom humor, de mau humor	to be in a good mood, in a bad mood
estar de cama	to be sick in bed
estar de castigo	to be grounded
estar de cócoras	to be crouching
estar de costas	to have one's back turned
estar de joelhos	to be on one's knees/to kneel down
estar de pé	to be standing
estar de visita	to be a visitor

3.3.8.2 Verbs which combine with *de*

abdicar de	to abdicate
aborrecer-se de	to become bored with (of)
abster-se de	to abstain from
abstrair-se de	to ignore (a thing)
abusar de	to abuse
acabar de (+ inf)	to finish
achar de	to think of (only used in questions)
afastar-se de	to distance oneself from
apear-se de	to get off of
aperceber-se de	to realize
apoderar-se de	to take control of
aproveitar-se de	to take advantage of
aproximar-se de	to get close to
armar-se de	to arm oneself with

arrepender-se de	to regret
assegurar-se de	to make sure of
atestar o depósito de/com	to fill the gas/petrol tank with
avisar de	to warn about
cansar-se de (+ inf)	to tire of
capacitar-se de	to convince oneself of
carecer de	to lack
chamar alguém de (Br)	to call (someone something)
cobrir de/com	to cover with
coibir-se de	to abstain from
condoer-se de	to be sorry for
constar de	to consist of
convencer alguém de	to convince someone of
corrigir-se de	to correct (such as a bad habit)
curar-se de	to recover from (an illness)
dar de (+ inf)	to decide to do something
datar de	to date from
decorrer de	to result from
deixar de (+ inf)	to stop or quit (+ gerund)
demitir-se de	to resign from
depender de	to depend on
depreender-se de	to infer from
desacostumar-se de	to no longer be accustomed to, to lose the habit of
descer de	to descend from, to get off
de(s)colar de	to take off from (aircraft)
desconfiar de	to distrust, to suspect
descrer de	to not believe (in)
desenvencilhar-se de	to get rid of
desfazer-se de	to rid oneself of
desistir de	to give up
despedir-se de	to say goodbye to
despojar-se de	to get rid of
destacar-se de	to stand out from
destoar de	to not match
desviar-se de	to veer from
diferir de	to differ from
discordar de	to disagree with
disfarçar-se de	to disguise oneself as
dispensar alguém de	to excuse someone from
dispor de	to possess
dissuadir alguém de	to dissuade someone from
distar de	to be at a distance from
distinguir de	to distinguish from
divorciar-se de	to divorce (somebody), get divorced from
duvidar de	to doubt

encarregar-se de	to be in charge of
entender de	to know about
envergonhar-se de	to be embarrassed about
escapar-se de	to escape from
escarnecer de	to make fun of
esquecer-se de	to forget about
falar de	to talk about
fartar-se de	to become fed up with
fazer de (+ noun)	to play the role of
gabar-se de (Pt)	to boast about
gostar de	to like
gozar de	to enjoy
ilibar de	to exonerate
impedir alguém de (+ inf)	to prevent someone from (+ gerund)
importar-se de (+ inf)	to mind
infestar de	to infest with
inhibir-se de	to be inhibited from
inteirar-se de	to find out about
lembrar-se de	to remember
libertar alguém de	to free someone from
mascarar-se de	to disguise oneself as
morrer de	to die of
mudar de (casa, roupa, dire(c)ção)	to move (as in housing), to change clothes, to change direction
munir-se de	to arm/equip oneself with
não passar de	to be no more than
necessitar de	to need
ocupar-se de	to dedicate oneself to
orgulhar-se de	to be proud of
padecer de	to suffer (from)
parar de (+inf)	to stop (+ gerund)
partir de	to leave
passar de	to be after (a certain time)
pensar de	to think of (only in questions)
perceber de	to know about
perder-se de	to lose sight of (someone)
precisar de	to need
prescindir de	to do without
proteger-se de	to protect oneself from
queixar-se de	to complain about
recompor-se de	to recover from
recordar-se de	to remember
reputar alguém de	to consider someone to be
ressentir-se de	to be resentful of

rir-se de	to laugh about
saber de	to know about
sair de	to leave
salpicar de /com	to sprinkle with, to splash with
separar de	to separate from
servir de	to serve as
servir-se de	to use
sofrer de	to suffer from
subsistir de	to survive on
surgir de	to come out of
suspeitar de	to suspect
tingir de	to dye (with something)
valer-se de	to take advantage of
vingar-se de	to avenge
viver de	to live on (as in food); to live off (earned or unearned income)
zombar de	to make fun of

3.3.9 *Desde*

Desde corresponds to English "from" in both space and time. It always indicates a movement from a point.

Examples:
Vim a pé desde minha casa até a universidade. (Br)
I came on foot from my house to the university.

Moro aqui desde 1977.
I have lived here since 1977.

3.3.10 *Diante de*

Diante de means "before" or "in front of" in space

Examples:
Cláudia colocou-se diante do espelho.
Claudia moved in front of the mirror.

O meu carro está diante de tua casa.
My car is in front of your house.

Note: *Diante* without *de* is used in some expressions to mean "from now on" in time

Example:
Daqui para diante não tolerarei os seus insultos.
From now on I will not tolerate your insults.

3.3.11 *Em*

Note: The preposition *em* joins in a contraction with the definite articles and the demonstrative adjectives and pronouns.

Examples:
No inverno chove muito.
In the winter it rains a lot.

Neste caso, devemos ter muito cuidado.
In this case, we should proceed with caution.

3.3.11.1 Basic uses with location

Em corresponds to the English preposition "in," "at" or "on," "inside (of)."

1. Containers

   Example:
   O meu porta-moedas está na bolsa.
   My wallet is in my purse.

2. Rooms

   Example:
   Comeremos na sala hoje.
   We will eat in the living room today.

3. Buildings

   Example:
   Havia uma exposição no Mosteiro dos Jerónimos.
   There was an exhibition in the Jeronimites Monastery.

4. Geographic locations

   Examples:
   O meu irmão mora no Algarve
   My brother lives in the Algarve.

   Eu gostaria de viver no estado de São Paulo.
   I would love to live in the state of São Paulo.

   Sempre há cobras neste parque nacional.
   There are many snakes in this National Park.

   Em Lisboa, há muitas casas de fado.
   In Lisbon there are many *fado* houses.

   Não há vida em Marte.
   There is no life on Mars.

   Note: The names of some cities and most countries are preceded by the definite article

Em with location	em casa	at home
	em casa de	in the home of
	na casa de	in the house of
	na cervejaria	at the beer bar
	na escola	at school
	na praia	on the beach/at the beach
	no bar	at the pub/café
	no cinema	at the theater/at the movies
	no teatro	at the theater
	no trabalho	at work

3.3.11.2 Basic uses with time

Periods of time meaning "during"

Example:
A Volta ao Mundo em Oitenta Dias.
Around the World in 80 Days.

1. With days and dates, including holidays

   Examples:
   Na segunda-feira, vamos ao Porto.
   On Monday we are going to Oporto.

   A guerra acabou no dia 13 de setembro.
   The war ended on September 13.

   No Natal come-se muito peru.
   At Christmas people eat a lot of turkey.

2. With months and seasons

   Examples:
   Vamos a Moçambique em Junho.
   We are going to Mozambique in June.

   No verão faz muito calor.
   It is very hot in summer.

3. With years

   Examples:
   Nasci em 1965.
   I was born in 1965.

   O Brasil tornou-se independente no ano de 1822.
   Brazil became independent in the year 1822.

4. With centuries

   Example:
   No século XXI, descobrir-se-á uma cura para o cancro. (Pt)
   In the twenty-first century, they will discover a cure for cancer.

Em with time expressions

de agora em diante	from now on
hoje em dia	nowadays
neste momento	in/at this moment
no futuro	in the future
no passado	in the past
no presente	in the present

Expressions with Em

crer em Deus	to believe in God
de quando em quando	once in a while
em breve	soon
em busca de	in search of
em carne viva	bare flesh (when the skin is scraped off)
em chamas	on fire
em confidência	in confidence
em dire(c)to	live (as in a broadcast)
em especial	in particular
em férias	on vacation
em ferida	wounded; with the skin scraped off
em festa	in celebration (this expression is used to describe a town when it celebrates its saint's feast: **Lisboa está em festa em Junho.** Lisbon celebrates its patron saint in June.)
em flor	in bloom
em função de	depending upon
em guerra	at war
em nome de	on behalf of, in the name of
em parte	in part
em paz	at peace, alone ("Deixa-me em paz" – "Leave me alone")
em princípio	hopefully
em resposta a	in response to
em segredo	in secret
em seguida	next
em todo caso	in any case
em transe	in a trance
em trânsito	in transit
em vão	in vain
em vez de	instead of
em virtude de	by virtue of, as a result of
fechar-se em copas	to keep one's mouth closed

na minha opinião	in my opinion
na qualidade de	as, in one's capacity as
no máximo	at the most
no melhor dos casos	in the best case, at best
no mínimo	at the least
no pior dos casos	in the worst case, at worst

Verbs which combine with *em*

acabar em	to end in
acertar em	to hit a target (also figuratively "to be on the mark")
acreditar em	to believe in
alistar-se em	to enlist in
andar em (Pt)	to frequent; to be enrolled in a degree program
apostar em	to bet on, to channel one's resources into
armar-se em + adj (Pt)	to pretend to be
aterrar em (Pt)	to land at (as for airplanes)
avaliar em	to appraise
avançar em	to progress in
basear-se em	to base oneself on
bater em	to hit (someone or something)
caminhar em	to walk along
caprichar em	to put special effort into
carregar em	to press (as in to apply pressure)
centrar-se em	to focus on
comparticipar em	to contribute money to
concordar em	to agree upon
confiar em	to trust
consentir em	to authorize, to allow
consistir em	to consist of
converter em	to transform into
crer em	to believe in
dar em	to become
decompor em	to divide into smaller parts
delegar em	to delegate to, deputize to
depositar em	to deposit in
desaguar em	to flow into
desembocar em	to flow into (usually of a river, but also including streets and other figurative meanings)
desfazer-se em	to overdo something

distinguir-se em	to distinguish oneself at (something)
embater em	to crash into
embrenhar-se em	to get lost in
empoleirar-se em	to perch upon
engalfinar-se em (Pt)	to get into a fight with
entrar em	to enter
espalhar-se em	to spread on, to spill on/over
esvair-se em	to drain into
exceder-se em	to surpass oneself at
falar em	to speak in (a language); to talk about
formar-se em	to get a degree in
hesitar em	to hesitate in
incorrer em	to commit (e.g. a mistake)
incutir em	to inculcate in
induzir em	to lead into
influir em	to influence
ingressar em	to join (e.g. a club)
insistir em	to insist upon
inspirar-se em	to find inspiration in
interferir em	to interfere in
investir em	to invest in
licenciar-se em	to get a college degree in (a subject)
matricular-se em	to enroll in
meditar em	to meditate on
mexer em	to touch
morder em	to bite on
negociar em	to deal in
pendurar em	to hang something on (something)
pendurar-se em	to hang onto
radicar-se em	to establish residence in, settle in
recair em	to fall back into
refletir em	to reflect upon, to ponder
refletir-se em	to reflect on (as in light)
reparar em	to notice
repercutir-se em	to have repercussions on
reprovar em	to fail at
rivalizar em	to rival in
tardar em	to be late in (doing something)
teimar em	to insist upon
transformar em	to transform into
transigir em	to give in (to a demand, etc.)
votar em	to vote on

3.3.12 *Entre*

Entre corresponds to the English "between" both in space and time and also figuratively.

Examples:
O meu escritório fica entre o do meu chefe e a saída.
My office is between my boss's and the exit.

Entre as duas e as três António telefonou quatro vezes. (Pt)
Between two and three Antonio called four times.

Estou indeciso entre ir ao cinema e jantar com os meus amigos.
I am undecided between going to the movies and dining with my
    friends.

Há sempre problemas entre irmãos.
There are always problems between siblings.

3.3.13 *Para* and *por*

Para and *por* are both equivalents for the English "for" but also have many other meanings and uses. The important difference is that *para* generally communicates movement (whether in time, in space, or figuratively) towards a fixed destination, goal or receiver, while *por* does not.

3.3.13.1   Basic uses of *Para*

1.   Purpose, aim; "in order to"

Examples:
Estudo para ser médico.
I am studying to become a doctor.

Para aprender português, se deve morar num país lusófono.
In order to learn Portuguese, one should live in a Portuguese-speaking
    country.

2.   Motion towards a specific destination

Example:
Vamos para Recife.
We are going to Recife.

3.   Recipient of an action

Example:
Trouxe um presente para você.
I brought a gift for you.

4. Use or suitability

Examples:

Este papel é muito bom para escrever cartas.
This paper is very good for writing letters.

Nos transportes públicos há sempre lugares reservados para mulheres grávidas, crianças, idosos e deficientes.
On public transportation there are always special seats reserved for pregnant women, children, seniors, and the disabled.

5. Deadlines or definite points in time

Example:

Este trabalho de casa é para manhã.
This homework is for tomorrow.

6. Time

Example:

São dez para as duas.
It's ten to two.

7. Compared with, considering

Examples:

Para professora, ela dá muitos erros.
For a teacher, she makes a lot of mistakes.

Ele é muito alto para um rapaz de cinco anos.
He is very tall for a ten year old.

8. To be about to, to be on the verge of

Example:

Estava para ir embora quando Rogério chegou.
I was about to leave when Rogerio arrived.

3.3.13.2   Expressions with *para*

de lá para cá, de um lado para o outro	back and forth
lá para as tantas [Pt]	very late
para dar e vender [Pt]	many, in abundance
para já	for now
para sempre	forever

3.3.13.3   Basic uses of *Por*

Note: *Por* combines in a contraction with the definite articles to form *pelo, pela, pelos, pelas*:

1. Motivation, reasons

   Examples:

   Chegamos atrasados por causa do trânsito.
   We arrived late because of the traffic.

   Eu só vim pela comida.
   I only came for the food.

   O pai fez muitos sacrifícios pelos filhos.
   The father sacrificed a great deal for his children.

2. Emotion or attitudes

   Example:

   Tenho grande admiração por seu irmão.
   I have great admiration for your brother.

3. Approximate time

   Example:

   Eu janto por volte das oito.
   I eat around eight.

4. Through or around a location

   Examples:

   Caminhei pelo Rossio toda a tarde.
   I walked around the Rossio Square [in Lisbon] all afternoon.

   Vai-se para França passando por Espanha.
   One gets to France by passing through Spain.

5. Duration of an action (it is often omitted or replaced by *durante*, especially in Portugal)

   Example:

   Estive lá por três anos.
   I was there for three years.

6. Before the agent in the passive voice

   Example:

   Viagens na Minha Terra **foi escrito por Almeida Garrett.**
   "Travels in My Country" was written by Almeida Garrett.

7. Substitution or exchange; "on behalf of"

   Example:

   Te dou mil reais por esse carro.
   I will give you one thousand reals for that car.

8. Rate; "per" (including percentage)

    Examples:
    Marcos nunca dirige a mais de cem quilómetros por hora.
    Marcos never drives faster than one hundred kilometers per hour.

    A inflação está a cinco por cento.
    The inflation rate is five percent.

9. Frequency of an action

    Example:
    A minha família janta fora uma vez por semana.
    My family dines out once a week.

10. Instead or in place of

    Example:
    Eu trabalhei pela Márcia porque ela estava doente.
    I worked for Marcia because she was sick.

3.3.13.4   Expressions with *por*

acabar por	to end up by (+ gerund)
ansiar por	"can't wait to"
apaixonar-se, estar apaixonado por alguém	to be passionate about, be mad about somebody
chamar por alguém	to call out for somebody
começar por	to start out by
dar por alguma coisa/alguém	to come to one's senses
dar-se por	to consider oneself to be
dividir por	to divide by
esforçar-se por	to strive to
esperar por alguém	to wait for someone
estar morto por	to be dying to (do something)
falar por falar	to speak for the sake of speaking
fazer pela vida (Pt)	to make a living
ficar-se por	to limit oneself to
interessar-se por	to become interested in
lutar por	to struggle for, to fight for
multiplicar por	to multiply by
olhar por	to look after
optar por	to opt for
passar por	to be thought to be something or someone you are not, pass yourself off as; to go through something/somebody
pelo menos (= ao menos)	at least

pelos vistos	apparently
perguntar por alguém	to ask for someone
por agora, por enquanto	for now
por certo	certainly
por conseguinte	therefore, so
por escrito	in writing
por fim	finally
por gosto	for the fun of it
por inteiro	totally
por isso	for that reason
por mim/ti . . .	as far as I/you (etc.) am/are concerned; for me/you (etc.)
por outro lado	on the other hand
por pouco	barely
por sorte	luckily
por último	finally, lastly
por um lado . . . por outro	on the one hand . . . on the other . . .
por/pelo amor de Deus	for the love of God
primar por	to distinguish for
recear por alguém	to be afraid for somebody
reger-se por	to follow (as in rules)
regozijar-se por	to be happy for
ser por	to be in favor of
suspirar por	to long for
tomar alguém por	to mistake someone for

3.3.14   *Sem*

Sem is used to express the English "without."

Examples:
Não saias de casa sem o guarda-chuva. (Pt)
Don't leave home without your umbrella.

O cliente foi-se embora sem pagar.
The customer left without paying.

3.3.15   *Sob*

Sob is used to express "under" in formal or literary discourse. In spoken discourse it is generally used figuratively. It is also used in the historical context to express "in the reign of."

Examples:
Sob o céu estrelado a cidade dormia em paz.
Under the starry sky, the city slept in peace.

Estou sob muita pressão por causa dos prazos a cumprir.
I am under a lot of pressure because of upcoming deadlines.

Sob Dom Manuel, desenvolveu-se o estilo manuelino.
The Manueline [architectural] style was developed under King
  Manuel.

3.3.16 *Sobre*

Sobre is used to express "on top of" and is used figuratively to mean
"about."

Examples:
Ela pôs os talheres de prata sobre a mesa para os limpar.
She placed the silver utensils on the table in order to clean them.

O convidado vai falar sobre as suas experiências médicas.
The guest speaker will talk about his medical experiments.

3.4 Prefixes and suffixes

3.4.1 Diminutives

Diminutive suffixes are used to denote smallness or to express affection
regarding an object, animal, or person, while augmentatives indicate
largeness. Both may be used literally or in a figurative sense.

   Diminutives are formed as follows. Note that final plural *–s* or *-es* is
always removed before adding the suffix and the suffix is then
pluralized:

1. For words ending in *–s* or *–z*, add the suffix *–inho* or *-inha*.
    rapaz > rapazinho
    boy > little boy

    voz > vozinha
    voice > little voice

    adeus > adeusinho
    goodbye > bye bye (in this case the diminutive indicates informality or
      affection)

2. For words ending in unstressed *–o* or *–a*, remove the final vowel before
    adding *-inho/-inha*.
    bolo > bolinho
    cake > little cake, cupcake

    casas > casinhas
    houses > little houses

porco > porquinho
pig > little pig, piglet

gato > gatinho
cat > kitty, kitten

3. If the words end in an unstressed *–e*, *–i*, or *–u*, add *–zinho*.
cidades > cidadezinhas
cities > villages

ave > avezinha
bird > birdie or little bird

4. If the word ends in a stressed vowel, diphthong, or any consonant other than *–s* or *–z*, then add *–zinho*.
peru > peruzinho
turkey > small turkey

limão > limãozinho
lemon > small lemon

hotel > hotelzinho
hotel > little hotel

hotéis > hoteizinhos
hotels > little hotels

5. For words ending in *–m*, change to *–n* before the suffix.
trem > trenzinho
train > little train

There are other suffixes used with certain words which express a specialized meaning but do not express affection.
These other suffixes include:

–acho
rio > riacho
river > creek

–icha
barba > barbicha
beard > little beard

–isco
chuva > chuvisco
rain > light rain

–ilho
pecado > pecadilho
sin > little sin

–ela
rua > ruela
street > alley

3.4.2 Augmentatives

Augmentative suffixes show either a large size or quantity, both literally and figuratively.

They may also have a negative connotation.

The most common suffixes are *–ão* for masculine and *–ona* for feminine words.

Words ending in a diphthong or a nasal take the suffix *–zão* or *–zona*.

carro > carrão
car > big car, or to show admiration

dinheiro > dinheirão
money > a lot of money

mulher > mulherona
woman > big woman (this has a negative connotation)

solteira > solteirona
single woman > spinster (this has a negative connotation)

Some words have specialized meanings and change gender when combining with the augmentative suffix:

---

a roupa > o roupão
clothes > a robe
um comilão
a glutton
um vidro > um vidrão
glass > a glass recycling receptacle
uma garrafa > um garrafão
bottle > five-liter jug
uma palavra > um palavrão
word > swear word
uma porta > um portão
door > gate

Other augmentative endings include:

–anzil
corpo > corpanzil
body > big body
–aréu
fogo > fogaréu
fire > big fire
–orra
cabeça > cabeçorra
head > big head

3.4.3 Professions, stores, and services

The names of many professions are formed by a suffix added to the product or task performed:

1. *-eiro*
    The ending *–eiro* is used for males and *–eira* for females while *–eiro* is also the neutral form.

banqueiro	banker
cabeleireiro	hairdresser
calceteiro	street paver
carpinteiro	carpenter
carteiro	mail carrier, postman
correeiro	leather worker
coveiro	gravedigger
cutileiro	knifemaker, cutler
engenheiro	engineer
fanqueiro	draper
ferreiro	blacksmith
garimpeiro	gold miner
livreiro	bookseller
pedreiro	stone mason
sapateiro	shoemaker or shoe repairman
toureiro	bullfighter

2. *-or*
    The form *–or* is used for males and *–ora* is used for females. The suffix *–or* is also the neutral form.

agricultor	farmer
cantor	singer
escritor	writer
escultor	sculptor
espectador	spectator
estivador	stower, docker, stevedore
historiador	historian
jogador	player
pintor	painter
prestidigitador	magician
silvicultor	forester
vendedor	seller, vendor

3. *-grafo*
    The form *–grafo* is used for males and *–grafa* is used for females. The suffix *–grafo* is also the neutral form:
    fotógrafo, coreógrafo, cineógrafo, etc.

4. *–ista*

The suffix *–ista* is used for both males and females and corresponds to the English –ist, especially in medical specialties:
jornalista, cardiologista, ecologista, etc.

Different from English are:
contista (short story writer)
romancista (novelist)
contabilista (accountant)

5. *–aria*

The names of stores in Portuguese are generally formed by adding the suffix *–aria* to the name of the product sold:

---

barba > barbearia
beard > barber shop

cerveja > cervejaria
beer > bar

droga > drogaria
drug > drug store (an old-fashioned corner drug store with toiletries, light hardware, etc.)

gelado > geladaria
ice cream > ice cream parlor

leite > leitaria
milk > dairy store

livro > livraria
book > bookstore

pão > padaria
bread > bakery

pastel > pastelaria
cake > bakery or pastry shop

sapato > sapataria
shoe > shoe store

3.5 Forms of address and treatment

3.5.1 Title and forms of address

Portuguese has two forms of address, one informal and one formal.
The informal pronoun "you" (second person) is expressed as *tu* (singular) and *vocês* (plural) in Portugal. In Brazil, while *tu* is used in some regions, the common forms are *você* (singular) and *vocês* (plural).

It is also important to note that *você* and *vocês* are conjugated like the third person while *tu* has its own conjugation (in Portugal, Lusophone Africa and southern Brazil).

The informal forms of address are used to address friends, family members, and children.

Portugal:
Tu nunca fazes o que eu te digo.
You never do what I tell you.

Vocês são brilhantes em tudo o que fazem.
You [pl] are brilliant in everything you do.

Brazil:
Você quer beber um suco?
Do you want to drink some juice?

Espero que você faça boa viagem.
I hope that you have a nice trip.

Onde é que tu vai no Natal (Santa Catarina)?
Where are you going for Christmas?

Note: The *você* form also exists in Portugal but it is more formal.

The formal forms of treatment are varied in both Portugal and Brazil and are usually related to the addressee's title. The masculine forms (with *o*) and the feminine forms (with *a*) are given for each.

Examples:
o senhor (sir/Mister)
a senhora (Madam/ma'am/Mrs.)
o senhor doutor, a senhora doutora (Doctor or anyone with a college degree)
o senhor engenheiro, a senhora engenheira (for those with a degree in engineering)
o senhor arquite(c)to, a senhora arquite(c)ta (architect)
o senhor professor, a senhora professora (teacher or professor)
o senhor doutor juiz, a senhora doutora juíza (judge)
o senhor dire(c)tor, a senhora dire(c)tora (supervisor/manager/director)
o senhor presidente, a senhora presidente (president or CEO)

A senhora podia fazer o favor de abrir a janela?
Could you open the window [to a woman]?

Os senhores professores não querem vir jantar connosco?
Would you [to several professors] like to come dine with us?

O senhor doutor pode ver a minha filha amanhã?
Doctor, could you see my daughter tomorrow?

3.5.2 Abbreviated titles

In written discourse, titles are generally abbreviated.

Sr. (senhor)	Sir, Mr.
Sra. (senhora)	Madam, Mrs., Miss, Ms.
Dra. (doutora)	Doctor (female)
Dr. (doutor)	Doctor (male)
D. (dona)	Mrs., Miss, Ms.
Ex.mo (excelentíssimo)	This form is used as a general salutation in formal letters and precedes the name or title of the addressee.
Ex.ma (excelentíssima)	Your excellency (female). See above.
Ilmo. (ilustríssimo)	You (very formal). This form is used as a salutation. In the case of a female addressee, "Ilma." is used.
V.Ex.cia (Vossa Excelência)	You (formal) within the body of the letter.
MI. (meritíssimo)	You (very formal). This would also be used as a salutation.
Prof. Doutor (Professor Doutor)	For a male with a Ph.D.
Prof.ª Doutora (Professora Doutora)	For a female with a Ph.D.

Two other forms of address which correspond to "Dear" are used in letters in the greeting and are not abbreviated:

Querido/Querida (more informal)
Caro/Cara (less formal)
Prezado/Prezada (more formal)

3.5.3 Closing expressions for letters

For informal letters, the following closings are used:
Teu amigo/ Tua amiga
Your friend

The following correspond to the English closure "Love,":
Beijos, Beijinhos
Kisses (for a member of the opposite sex, female friends, or for family members)

Abraços, Um abraço,
Hugs, A hug (for friends)

For formal letters, the following correspond to the English "Sincerely," "Faithfully," or "Yours truly,":

Com os meus cumprimentos,
With my compliments,

Com os meus melhores cumprimentos,
With my best compliments,

Atenciosamente,
Attentively,

3.5.4 Telephone communication

The following greetings correspond to the English "Hello" when answering the telephone:

Portugal:
— **Estou sim?**   — **Está?**

Brazil:
— **Alô?**

Note: in Mozambique and Guinea Bissau, "Alô?" is also used.

In Portuguese, the request to speak with a party is more formal than in American English. Thus one would not say: "Is Marcos there?", but instead:

Daqui fala Luís Valente. Podia falar com Marcos?
This is Luís Valente. Could I speak with Marcos?

Telephone conversations are closed with the following expressions:

Até logo (Until later)
Adeus/Tchau (Good-bye)
Boa-noite, Boa-tarde, Bom-dia (Good night, Good afternoon, Good day)
Com licença (With your permission)

The following is a model of a typical formal telephone conversation.

O Sr. Gomes:	*atende o telefone* Estou?
A Sra. Castro:	Estou sim, bom-dia. Daqui fala Luísa Castro. Podia falar com o Sr. Dire(c)tor?
O Sr. Gomes:	Não está neste momento. Deseja deixar recado?
A Sra. Castro:	Não, obrigada. Ligarei mais tarde.
O Sr. Gomes:	Com certeza. Bom-dia.
A Sra. Castro:	Bom-dia. Com licença.
Mr. Gomes:	*answers the telephone* Hello?
Mrs. Castro:	Hello. This is Luisa Castro. May I speak with the Director?

Mr. Gomes:	He is not here at the moment. May I take a message?
mrs. Castro:	No, thank you. I'll call back later.
Mr. Gomes:	OK. Good-bye.
Mrs. Castro:	Good-bye.

Note. The following expressions are customary in telephone conversations:

É engano.	You have the wrong number.
É o próprio. É a própria.	Speaking.
Está ocupado.	The line is busy.
Podia ligar-me a ———?	Could you connect me with/ to ———?

3.6   Idiomatic expressions

3.6.1   Proverbs

English equivalents are given when applicable. If there is no English proverb equivalent, then an approximate translation and explanation are given.

A cavalo dado não se olha o dente. (Pt)	Don't look a gift horse in the mouth.
A esperança é a última que morre! (Br); A esperança é a última a morrer. (Pt)	Hope dies last.
Enquanto há vida, há esperança.	While there is life, there is hope.
A galinha da vizinha é sempre melhor do que a minha.	The grass is always greener on the other side of the fence (lit. "The neighbor's chicken is always better than mine").
Água mole em pedra dura, tanto bate até que fura.	Soft water on hard rock eventually breaks it, i.e. insistence will wear one down.
Antes tarde do que nunca. (Br); Mais vale tarde do que nunca. (Pt)	Better late than never.
Bem prega Frei Tomás: fazei o que ele diz, não o que ele faz. (Pt) Faz o que eu digo, não o que eu faço. (Br)	Don't do as I do, do as I say (lit. "Father Thomas preaches well, do as he says, not as he does").
Cada um dá o que tem, a mais não é obrigado.	Every person gives what he/she has and is not obligated to do anything else, i.e. one should give in proportion to what one has.

Cada cabeça, sua sentença.	To each his own (lit. "Every head, its own sentence").
Cada um por si, Deus por todos. (Pt)	Every man for himself and Devil take the hindmost (lit. "God for all").
Cachorro que ladra não morde. (Br); **Cão que ladra não morde.** (Pt)	Barking dogs don't bite.
De Espanha, nem bom vento, nem bom casamento. (Pt)	From Spain neither good winds nor good marriages, i.e. nothing good comes from Spain.
De grão em grão, a galinha enche o papo. (Br) **Grão a grão, enche a galinha o papo.** (Pt)	If you look after the pennies the pounds will look after themselves (lit. "Grain by grain, the hen fills her stomach").
De pequenino se torce o pepino.	From the time they are little, cucumbers are twisted, i.e. good habits must be instilled at a young age.
Deus ajuda quem cedo madruga. (Br)	God helps those who wake up early.
Deus escreve direito por linhas tortas. or **Há males que vêm por bem.** (Pt); **Há males que vêm para bem.** (Br)	Every cloud has a silver lining (lit. "God writes straight with crooked lines," i.e. there are bad things that occur for a good reason; everything happens for a reason).
Devagar se vai ao longe.	If you walk slowly, you'll walk far, i.e. if you persevere you'll eventually attain your goals.
Diz-me com quem andas, e te direi quem és. (Pt)	Birds of a feather flock together (lit. "Tell me whom you go with, and I will tell you who you are").
Dos fracos não reza a história. (Pt)	History does not report the actions of the defeated.
Em Abril, águas mil. (Pt)	In April, a thousand rains.
Em casa de ferreiro, espeto de pau. (Pt); **Em casa de ferreiro, o espeto é de pau.** (Br)	In the blacksmith's house, stick of wood, i.e. you don't do at home what you do at work.
Em Roma, sê como os romanos. (Pt)	When in Rome, do as the Romans do.
Em terra de cegos, quem tem olho é rei. (Pt); **Em terra de cego, quem tem um olho é rei.** (Br)	In the kingdom (lit. "land") of the blind the one-eyed man is king.
Entre marido e mulher não metas a colher. (Pt) **Entre marido e mulher não se mete a colher.** (Br)	Between husband and wife, don't place a spoon, i.e. don't interfere in a couple's affairs.

Gaivotas em terra, tempestade no mar. (Pt)	Seagulls on land show storms at sea.
Gato escaldado da água fria tem medo. (Pt); Gato escaldado tem medo de água fria. (Br)	Once bitten, twice shy (lit. "Cat once scalded is afraid of cold water").
Homem prevenido vale por dois.	A trained man (soldier) is worth two.
Ladrão que rouba a ladrão tem cem anos de perdão. (Pt); Ladrão que rouba de ladrão, tem cem anos de perdão. (Br)	The thief who steals from a thief receives 100 years of pardon, i.e. it is not wrong to steal from a thief.
Longe dos olhos, longe do coração.	Out of sight, out of mind (lit. "Far from the eyes, far from the heart").
Mais vale só que mal acompanhado.	Better alone than in bad company.
Mais vale um pássaro na mão do que dois a voar.	A bird in the hand is worth two in the bush (lit. "flying").
Março, marçagão, de manhã Inverno, de tarde Verão. (Pt)	In March, the mornings are like winter and the afternoons like summer.
Não há domingo sem missa, nem segunda sem preguiça. (Pt)	There are no Sundays without mass, nor Mondays without laziness.
Não há mulher sem graça, nem poeta sem cachaça. (Br)	There is no woman without grace and no poet without sugar cane liquor.
Não se pode tocar os sinos e andar na procissão. (Pt)	You can't ring the bells and walk in the procession, i.e. you can't do two things at once.
Nem tudo o que brilha é ouro.	All that glitters is not gold.
Nunca deixe para amanhã o que você pode fazer hoje. (Br); Não deixes para amanhã o que podes fazer hoje. (Pt)	Never put off until tomorrow what you can do today.
O pior surdo é aquele que não quer ouvir. (Pt); O pior cego é o que não quer ver. (Br)	None so deaf as those who won't hear (lit. "None so blind as those who won't see").
O segredo é a alma do negócio.	Silence is golden (lit. "Secrecy is the soul of business").
Para bom entendedor, meia palavra basta.	For the good listener, half a word is enough.
Quanto mais alto se vai, de mais alto se cai. (Pt)	The taller they are, the harder they fall (lit. "The higher you go, the further you fall").

Quanto mais se tem, mais se quer.	The more you have, the more you want.
Quem cala, consente.	Silence gives consent.
Quem canta, seus males espanta. (Pt)	He who sings scares away his troubles.
Quem cedo madruga, dorme à tarde. (Br)	He who gets up early has to take a nap in the afternoon.
Quem despreza, quer comprar. (Pt)	He who criticizes, covets.
Quem ama o feio, bonito lhe parece. (Br); Quem feio ama, bonito lhe parece. (Pt)	Beauty is in the eye of the beholder (lit. "She who loves an ugly person, he seems handsome to her").
Quem não arrisca, não petisca. (Pt)	Nothing ventured, nothing gained.
Quem não deve, não teme.	He who has done nothing wrong should not fear to be probed.
Quem não tem cão, caça com gato.	He who doesn't have a dog, hunts with a cat, i.e. one must make the best of what's available.
Quem nunca comeu melado, quando come se labuza. (Br)	He who has never tried molasses, when he does try it gets it all over himself, i.e. can't have enough of it.
Quem se mete por atalhos, não se livra de trabalhos. (Pt)	If you take a short cut, you do not escape trouble, i.e. the shortest way is not always the easiest.
Quem ri por último, ri melhor.	He who laughs last, laughs best.
Quem semeia ventos, colhe tempestades. (Pt)	As you sow, so shall you reap.
Quem tem boca, vai dar a Roma.	If you have a mouth, you will get to Rome, i.e. if you can ask questions, you can find your way.
Quem tem telhados de vidro não atira pedras ao vizinho.	People who live in glass houses shouldn't throw stones.
Quem vê cara, não vê coração. (Br); Quem vê caras, não vê corações. (Pt)	You can't judge a book by its cover (lit. "He who sees faces cannot see hearts").
Roma e Pavia não se fizeram num (só) dia. (Pt)	Rome wasn't built in a day.
Se não queres ser lobo, não lhe vistas a pele. (Pt)	If you don't want to be a wolf, don't dress as one, i.e. don't act as one.
Tal pai, tal filho.	Like father, like son.

Todos os caminhos vão dar a Roma.	All roads lead to Rome.
Tudo o que arde, cura, e o que aperta, segura. (Br)	Everything that burns, heals, and everything that tightens, secures.
Voz de burro não chega ao céu. (Br); Vozes de burro não chegam ao céu. (Pt)	The voice of a donkey does not reach heaven, i.e. common people's voices do not reach heaven's ears.

3.6.2   Metaphors

[um] Abacaxi. (Br)	A big or thorny problem.
Amigo de Peniche. (Pt)	A friend of Peniche, i.e. a false or non–dependable friend who doesn't come through when you need him/her. (Peniche is a town on the peninsula of Cabo Carvoeiro, known for its beaches and as a summer resort.)
[ser uma] Amostra de gente. (Pt)	A sample of people, i.e. (to be) small.
[ser um] Bom garfo.	A good fork, i.e. (to be) a gourmet.
[ser um] Bota de elástico. (Pt)	A rubber boot, i.e. (to be) square or old-fashioned.
[ser um(a)] Cabeça de alho chocho. (Pt)	A head of stale garlic, i.e. (to be) scatterbrained or forgetful.
Cada macaco no seu galho.	Each monkey on its own branch, i.e. every person in his own place.
Estar de saco cheio. (Br)	(To be) fed up with something, (to have) no more patience with something/somebody.
Em cascos de rolha (Pt); Onde o diabo perdeu as botas. (Br)	Where there are pieces of cork / Where the devil lost his boots, i.e. very far away.
Entre a espada e a parede.	Between a sword and a wall, i.e. between a rock and a hard place.
Falar pelos cotovelos. (Br); [ser um(a)] Fala-barato. (Pt)	(To be) a chatterbox.
Favas contadas. (Pt)	Counted beans, i.e. in the bag.
[uma] História do arco da velha.	A tall tale.
[um(a)] Pãozinho sem sal. (Pt)	(To be) bread without salt, i.e. dull.

[um(a)] Pau de virar tripas. (Pt)	A stick to stir tripe with, i.e. very skinny.
[um(a)] Pau mandado. (Pt)	A piece of wood, i.e. lifeless or devoid of will.
[um(a)] Rato de biblioteca.	A library mouse, i.e. a bookworm.
[um(a)] Santo de pau carunchoso. (Pt)	A saint made of rotten wood, i.e. a fake saint.
[um(a)] Unha de fome.	A nail of hunger, i.e. stingy.
[um] Zero à esquerda.	A zero to the left of the first digit of a given number, i.e. really useless or bad at something.

3.6.3   Verbal expressions

Andar com o credo na boca. (Pt)	To go with the creed in one's mouth, i.e. to be anxious and therefore always praying for a positive outcome.
Apanhar alguém com a boca na botija/em flagrante delito. (Pt)	To catch someone with their mouth on the bed warmer/in flagrante delicto, i.e. to catch someone in the act.
Arrastar a asa (a uma mulher). (Pt)	To drag a woman's wing, i.e. to seduce a woman.
Chegar a vias de facto. (Pt)	To argue with someone so heatedly that you get physical.
Dar zebra. (Br)	To go wrong or fall through.
Estar nas suas sete quintas. (Pt)	To be on one's seven farms, i.e. to be in seventh heaven.
Estar careca de saber [alguma coisa]. (Br)	To know something all too well.
Eu sou mais eu. (Br)	I alone but I (i.e. I believe in myself, I have great confidence).
Fazer jogo de cintura. (Br)	To make a yoke of one's belt, i.e. attempt to solve a delicate problem with great diplomacy and skill, at times by going around the obstacle.
Fazer o ninho atrás da orelha a alguém. (Pt)	To make the nest behind someone's ear, i.e. to try to seduce someone.
Lançar o barro à parede.	To throw the clay at the wall, i.e. to test the waters.
Lavar a égua. (Br)	To wash the mare, i.e. to eat a lot or enjoy greatly.

Não levar desaforo para casa. (Br)	Not to take any offense home, i.e. to settle matters when they arise.
Não ser ouvido nem achado. (Pt)	To not be heard or found, i.e. to not be consulted.
[É] Pegar ou largar.	Take it or leave it.
Passar pelas brasas. (Pt) / **Cochilar.** (Br)	To walk over coals (Pt), i.e. to doze off or to take a brief nap; to doze. (Br)
Pregar aos peixes. (Pt)	To preach to the fish, i.e. say something that falls on deaf ears.
Procurar agulha em palheiro.	To look for a needle in a haystack.
Puxar a brasa à sua sardinha.	To blow the heat on the coals under your sardines, i.e. to look out for your own interests.
Quando as galinhas tiverem dentes. (Pt)	When chickens grow teeth, i.e. never.
Sair o tiro pela culatra a alguém. (Pt)	To make something backfire on someone.
Se correr o bicho pega, se ficar o bicho come. (Br); **Preso por ter cão, preso por não ter.** (Pt)	If you run the animal will get you, if you stay still, it will eat you. (Br); caught for having a dog, caught for not (having one), i.e. damned if you do, damned if you don't.
Soltar a franga. (Br)	To let the hen go free, i.e. to let go of one's inhibitions, revealing a gaudy, exaggerated self.
Vai ver se estou na esquina. / Vai catar coquinho. (Br) / **Vai pentear macaco.**	Go see if I am over there, i.e. leave me alone.

3.6.4 Similes

Similes are usually preceded by the verb *ser*, although they can also occur with a different verb.

Cheio que nem um ovo.	Full as an egg.
Chorar que nem uma Madalena	To cry like Mary Magdalene.
Claro como água.	Clear as water.
Correr que nem uma lebre. (Pt)	To run as fast as a hare.
Feio que nem um trovão. (Pt)	Uglier than thunder.

Fumar que nem uma chaminé.	To smoke like a chimney.
Gordo como uma pipa. (Pt)	Fat as a barrel.
Lento que nem uma tartaruga/um caracol.	Slow as a turtle/a snail.
Mau como as cobras. (Pt)	Evil as snakes.
Sorrateiro que nem uma raposa. (Pt)	Cunning as a fox.
Surdo que nem uma porta.	Deaf as a doorknob (lit. door).
Teimoso que nem um burro.	Stubborn as a mule.

3.7 Adjectives

3.7.1 Adjectives pertaining to countries and towns

Portuguese, like all Romance languages, has special adjectives for inhabitants and products from different countries and towns.

It is important to note that national and regional adjectives are not capitalized in Portuguese.

3.7.1.1 Portugal (no article) -português

Regions

Origin	Adjective
Algarve (m)	algarvio
Alentejo (m)	alentejano
Estremadura (f)	estremenho
Minho (m)	minhoto
Beira Interior, Beira Litoral (f)	beirão, beirense
Trás-os-Montes (m, pl)	transmontano
Norte (m)	nortenho
Açores (m, pl)	açoriano
Madeira (f)	madeirense
Douro (m)	duriense

Cities

Lisboa	lisboeta, alfacinha
Porto	portuense, portista
Braga	bracarense
Coimbra	coimbrão
Évora	eborense
Viana do Castelo	vianense

Arcos de Valdevez	arcuense
Famalicão	famalicense
Vila do Conde	vilacondense
Penafiel	penafidelense
Vila Real	vila-realense
Lamego	lamecense
Viseu	visiense
Estremoz	estremocense
Portimão	portimonense
Loulé	louletano
Olhão	olhanense
Ponta Delgada	micaelense

3.7.1.2 Brasil-brasileiro

Regions

Nordeste	nordestino
Rio Grande do Sul	gaúcho
São Paulo	paulista
Minas Gerais	mineiro
Mato Grosso	matogrossense
Pernambuco	pernambucano
Paraíba	paraibenense
Bahia (f)	bahiano
Ceará	cearense
Goiás	goianense
Maranhão	maranhaense
Rio de Janeiro (m)	fluminense

Cities

Rio de Janeiro	carioca
São Paulo	paulistano
Porto Alegre	porto-alegrense
Curitiba	curitibano
Paraíba	paraíbano

3.7.1.3 Lusophone Africa

Angola	angolano
Moçambique	moçambicano
Cabo Verde	cabo-verdiano
São Tomé e Príncipe	são-tomense
Guiné Bissau (f)	guineense

3.7.1.4 Other nationalities

All regular feminine forms of the adjectives are formed by adding –*a* or changing the final –*o* to –*a*. All irregular feminine forms are given.

Afganistão (m)	afegão, afegã
África do Sul (f)	sul-africano
Albânia (f)	albanês, albanesa
Alemanha (f)	alemão, alemã (the plural is *alemães,* *alemãs*)
Arábia Saudita (f)	saudita or árabe (same form for both m and f)
Argélia (f)	argelino
Argentina (f)	argentino
Áustria (f)	austríaco
Bélgica (f)	belga (for both m and f)
Birmânia (f)	birmanês, birmanesa
Bolívia (f)	boliviano
Bósnia (f)	bósnio
Bulgária (f)	búlgaro
Camboja (m)	cambojano
Canadá (m)	canadiano (Pt), canadense (Br) (the f is also *canadense*)
Chile (m)	chileno
China (f)	chinês, chinesa
Chipre (m)	cipriota (for both m and f)
Colômbia (f)	colombiano
Coreia do Norte (f)	norte-coreano
Coreia do Sul (f)	sul-coreano
Costa Rica (f)	costa-riquenho
Croácia (f)	croata (for both m and f)
Cuba (f; no article)	cubano
Dinamarca (f)	dinamarquês, dinamarquesa
Egip(t)o (m)	egípcio
Equador (m)	equatoriano
Escócia (f)	escocês, escocesa
Eslováquia (f)	eslovaco
Eslovénia (f)	esloveno
Espanha (f)	espanhol
Andaluzia (f)	andaluz
Catalúnia (f)	catalão, catalã
Estremadura (f)	estremenho
Galiza (f)	galego
País Basco (m)	basco
Estados Unidos (m. pl)	norte-americano
Nova Iorque	novo-iorquino

Etiópia (f)	etíope (for both m and f)
Filipinas (f, pl)	filipino
Finlândia (f)	finlandês, finlandesa
França (f; no article in Pt)	francês, francesa
Paris	parisiense (the f; is also *parisiense*)
País de Gales (m)	galês, galesa
Geórgia (f)	georgiano
Grã-Bretanha (f)	britânico
Londres	londrino
Grécia (f)	grego
Guatemala (f)	guatemalteco
Holanda (f)	holandês, holandesa
Honduras (f, pl)	hondurenho
Hungria (f)	húngaro
Índia (f)	indiano
Indonésia (f)	indonésio
Inglaterra (f)	inglês, inglesa
Irão/Irã (Br) (m)	iraniano
Iraque (m)	iraquiano
Irlanda (f)	irlandês, irlandesa
Islândia (f)	islandês, islandesa
Israel (no article)	israelita (for both m and f) (Pt); israelense (Br)
Itália (f)	italiano
Japão (m)	japonês, japonesa
Jugoslávia (f)	jugoslavo
Líbano (m)	libanês, libanesa
Libéria (f)	liberiano
Líbia (f)	líbio/libanês, libanesa
Luxemburgo (m)	luxemburguês, luxemburguesa
Malásia (f)	malaio
Malta (no article)	maltês, maltesa
Marrocos (no article)	marroquino
Mauritânia (f)	mauritânio
México (m)	mexicano
Micronésia (f)	micronésio
Namíbia (f)	namíbio
Nepal (m)	nepalês, nepalesa
Nicaragua (f)	nicaraguense (the f is also nicaraguense)
Nigéria (f)	nigeriano
Noruega (f)	norueguês, norueguesa
Nova Caledónia (f)	novo-caledonês, nova-caledonesa
Nova Zelândia (f)	novo-zelandês, nova-zelandesa (Br)/neo-zelandês (Pt)
Panamá (m)	panamenho
Paquistão (m)	paquistanês, paquistanesa

Paraguai (m)	paraguaio
Peru (m)	peruano
Polónia (Pt)/Polônia (Br) (f)	polaco (Pt)/polonês, polonesa (Br)
Porto Rico (no article)	porto-riquenho
Quénia (m)	queniano
República Checa (f)	checo
Roménia (Pt)/ Romênia (Br) (f)	romeno
Rússia (f)	russo
Moscovo	moscovita
Salvador (m)	salvadorenho
Senegal (m)	senegalês, senegalesa
Serra Leone (f)	serra-leonês, serra-leonesa
Síria (f)	sírio
Somália (f)	somalês, somalesa
Sudão (m)	sudanês, sudanesa
Suécia (f)	sueco
Suíça (f)	suíço
Suriname (m)	surinamês, surinamesa
Tailândia (f)	tailandês, tailandesa
Tibete (m)	tibetano
Timor-Leste (m in Br, no article in Pt)	timorense (for both m and f)
Tunísia (f)	tunísio
Turquia (f)	turco
Uruguai (m)	uruguaio
Venezuela (f)	venezuelano
Vietname (Pt), Vietnã (Br) (m)	vietnamita (for both m and f).
Zaire (m)	zairiano/zairense
Zâmbia (f)	zambiano

3.7.1.5 Other descriptive adjectives: continents and geographic regions

América	americano
América do Norte	norte-americano
América do Sul	sul-americano
África	africano
Austrália	australiano
Ásia	asiático
América Latina	latino-americano
Europa	europeu, europeia (Pt)/européia (Br)

Oceans and seas	Oceano	Atlântico	Atlantic Ocean
		Índico	Indian Ocean
		Pacífico	Pacific Ocean
	Mar	Mediterrânico	Mediterranean
		Morto	Dead Sea
		Vermelho	Red Sea
		Cáspio	Caspian Sea
		Salgado	Salten Sea

3.8 Proper names

Portuguese usually translates foreign proper nouns when possible.
There is a larger variety of proper names left in the original language
in Brazil than in Portugal, as the latter is more strict in the use
of only historically Portuguese names and traditional
spelling.

3.8.1 The Ancient Greek world

Afrodite e Eros	Aphrodite and Eros
Alexandre	Alexander
Aquiles	Achilles
Ariana	Ariadne
Aristófanes	Aristophanes
Aristóteles	Aristotle
Arquimedes	Archimedes
Artemísia	Artemis
Atena	Athena
Deméter	Demeter
Dionísio	Dionysus
Édipo	Oedipus
Esopo	Aesop
Ésquilo	Aeschylus
Euclides	Euclid
Eurídice	Eurydice
Eurípides	Euripides
Febo	Phoebus
Hermes	Hermes

Homero	Homer
Leandro	Leander
Orfeu	Orpheus
Pitágoras	Pythagoras
Platão	Plato
Ulisses e Penélope	Ulysses and Penelope
Urano	Uranus
Xenofonte	Xenophon

3.8.2 The Ancient Roman world

Adriano	Hadrian
Aníbal	Hannibal
Apolo	Apollo
Augusto	Augustus
Baco	Bacchus
Boécio	Boethius
Cartago	Carthage
Catão	Cato
Cícero	Cicero
Cipião	Scipio
Cleópatra	Cleopatra
Cupido	Cupid
Gaio e Tibério Graco, os (irmãos) Gracos	Gaius and Tiberius Gracchus, the Gracchi
Hércules	Hercules
Horácio	Horace
Júlio César	Julius Caesar
Júpiter	Jupiter
Marco António	Mark Antony
Marte	Mars
Mercúrio	Mercury
Minerva	Minerva
Nero	Nero
Ovídio	Ovid
Plínio	Pliny
Plutão	Pluto
Saturno	Saturn
Tito Lívio	Livy or Titus Livius
Vénus	Venus
Vulcano	Vulcan

3.8.3 The Bible

Abel	Abel
Adão	Adam
André	Andrew
Belém	Bethlehem
Bíblia	Bible
Caín	Cain
Deus	God
Eva	Eve
Herodes	Herod
Isaías	Isaiah
Jeová	Jehova
Jerusalém	Jerusalem
Jesus Cristo	Jesus Christ
João Baptista	John the Baptist
Jonas	Jonah
José	Joseph
Josué	Joshua
Lucas	Luke
Madalena	Mary Magdalene
Moisés	Moses
Nazaré	Nazareth
Noé	Noah
o Messias	the Messiah
Pôncio Pilatos	Pontius Pilate
Raquel	Rachel
Rute	Ruth
Saba	Sheba
Satanás	Satan
Saúl	Saul
Sião	Zion

3.8.4 The medieval and Renaissance world

A Reconquista	The Reconquest
caravelas	caravels
Cristóvão Colombo	Christopher Columbus
as Descobertas/os Descobrimentos	the Discoveries
estilo Manuelino	Manueline style
Henrique, o Navegador	Henry the Navigator
Luís de Camões	Luis Camoens
Lutero	Luther

Magalhães	Magellan
Maquiavel	Machiavelli
Miguel Ângelo	Michelangelo
Moamed	Mohammed
Petrarca	Petrarch
São Tomás de Aquino	Saint Thomas Aquinas

3.8.5 Contemporary personal names

Afonso	Alphonse
Alberto	Albert
Alexandra	Alexandra
Alexandre	Alexander
Ana	Anna, Anne
André	Andrew
Andreia	Andrea
Ângelo	Angel
Antônio (Br)/ António (Pt)	Anthony
Catarina	Catherine, Kathleen
Chico	Francis
Conceição	Conception
Cristina	Christina
Eduardo	Edward
Estêvão	Steven/Stephen
Fernando	Ferdinand
Francisca	Frances
Francisco	Francis, Frank
Frederico	Frederick
Haroldo	Harold
Helena	Helena, Helen, Ellen
Henrique	Henry
Inês	Agnes
Isabel	Elizabeth
Jaime	James
João	John
Jorge	George
José	Joseph
Júlia	Julia
Julião, Júlio	Julian
Leonor	Eleanor
Lúcia	Lucy
Luís	Luis

Luísa	Louise
Marco	Mark
Margarida	Margaret
Maria	Mary
Mariana	Mary Ann
Marta	Martha
Miguel	Michael
Patrícia	Patricia
Patrício	Patrick
Paulo	Paul
Pedro	Peter
Rafael	Raphael
Ricardo	Richard
Ronaldo	Ronald
Sara	Sarah
Sofia	Sophie
Susana	Susan
Teresa	Theresa
Timóteo	Timothy
Tomás	Thomas
Vítor	Victor

3.8.6 Names of persons without close English equivalents. Please note that there are many more, in particular in Brazil and Lusophone Africa.

Ascensão
Bela (f)
Branca
Céu
Clotilde
Filomena
Leonilde
Marisa
Rafaela
Rodrigo
Rui
Sílvia
Silvina
Tiago

3.8.7 Cities, islands, states and counties

3.8.7.1 Europe

Amsterdão (Pt) / Amsterdã (Br)	Amsterdam
Antióquia	Antioch
Antuérpia	Antwerp
Atenas	Athens
Avinhon	Avignon
Baviera	Bavaria
Belgrado	Belgrade
Berlim	Berlin
Berna	Bern
Bona	Bonn
Bordéus	Bordeaux
Borgonha	Burgundy
Bruxelas	Brussels
Colónia	Cologne
Copenhaga	Copenhagen
Cornualha	Cornwall
Córsega	Corsica
Cracóvia	Krakov
Edinburgo	Edinburgh
Estocolmo	Stockholm
Estrasburgo	Strasburg
Flandres	Flanders
Florença	Florence
Friburgo	Freiburg
Gante	Ghent
Gasconha	Gascony
Genebra	Geneva
Génova	Genoa
Hamburgo	Hamburg
Haya	The Hague
Ilhas Baleares	Balearic Islands
Londres	London
Lovaina	Louvain
A Madeira	The Madeira archipelago
Mântua	Mantua–Mantova
Marselha	Marseilles
Milão	Milan
Moscovo (Pt) / Moscou (Br)	Moscow
Munique	Munich
Nápoles	Naples

Os Açores	The Azores (archipelago)
Pádua	Padua
Praga	Prague
Provença	Provence
Reikiavic	Reykjavík
Rodes	Rhodes
Roma	Rome
Roterdão	Rotterdam
Ruão	Rouen
Sabóia	Savoy
São Pitersburgo	Saint Petersburg
São Sebastião	San Sebastian
Sardenha	Sardinia
Saxónia	Saxony
Sevilha	Seville
Sicília	Sicily
Sófia	Sofia
Turim	Turin
Varsóvia	Warsaw
Veneza	Venice
Versalhes	Versailles
Viena	Vienna

3.8.7.2   Africa

Benguela	Bengal
O Cairo	Cairo
A Cidade do Cabo	Cape Town
A Ilha de Santiago	Santiago Island
A Ilha do Sal	Salt Island
Joanesburgo	Johannesburg
Kinchassa	Kinshasa
Tânger	Tangiers
Túnis	Tunis

3.8.7.3   North America

a Flórida	Florida
Filadélfia	Philadelphia
Luisiana	Louisiana
Nova Escócia	Nova Scotia
Nova Jersey	New Jersey
Nova Orleãs	New Orleans
Nova York	New York

Novo México	New Mexico
Pensilvânia	Pennsylvania
Santa Bárbara	Santa Barbara
São Francisco	San Francisco

3.8.7.4 Asia

Calcutá	Calcutta
Cantão	Canton
Nova Déli	New Delhi
Pequim	Peking/Beijing
Seúl	Seoul
Singapura	Singapore
Tóquio	Tokyo

3.8.7.5 Latin America

As Bahamas	The Bahamas
Brasília	Brasilia
As Caraíbas (Pt)/	The Caribbean
O Caribe (Br)	Islands
As Ilhas Malvinas	The Falkland Islands
Santiago do Chile	Santiago
São Salvador	San Salvador

3.8.7.6 Middle and Far East

Amã	Amman
Bagdade	Bagdad
Damasco	Damascus
Estambul	Istanbul
Jerusalém	Jerusalem
Meca	Mecca
Teérão (Pt)/Téerã (Br)	Tehran

3.8.8 Rivers

Amazonas	Amazon
Mississipi	Mississippi
Misuri	Missouri
Nilo	Nile
Reno	Rhine
Sena	Seine
Tames	Thames
Tejo	Tagus

3.8.9 Mountains

Os Alpes	Alps
Os Apalaches	Appalachians
Os Apeninos	Apennines
As Montanhas Rochosas	The Rocky Mountains
Os Pirinéus	Pyrenees
A Serra da Estrela	Estrela Mountains
A Serra Nevada	Sierra Nevada
Os Andes	The Andes

3.9 Abbreviations and acronyms

Abbreviations and acronyms are widely used in the Portuguese-speaking world. Abbreviations, unless otherwise noted, are pronounced as if they were words. Those that are pronounced letter by letter are marked with an asterisk. For personal titles refer to section 3.5.2.

3.9.1 Common abbreviations

a.C.*	antes de Cristo	B.C.
Apdo.	Apartado	Post Office Box
Av.	Avenida	Avenue
Bac.	Bacharelato	3-year college degree (in Portugal)
C.P.*	Caminhos de Ferro Portugueses	Portuguese Railways
cap.	capítulo	chapter
cfr.	confronte-se	compare
Cia.	Companhia	Company
cta.	conta	account
cte.	corrente	checking/current
D.	Dom	Mister
D.ª	Dona	Ms., Miss, Mrs.
d.C.*	depois de Cristo	A.D.
E	Este	East
exp.	exemplo	example
Fr.	Frei	Fray, Brother
G.N.R.*	Guarda Nacional Republicana	National Guard

id.	idem	idem
Lic.	Licenciatura	4-year college degree
Mons.	Monsenhor	Monseigneur
N	Norte	North
N.ª S.ª	Nossa Senhora	Our Lady
N.B.	Nota Bene	Please Note
NE	Nordeste	Northeast
NO	Noroeste	Northwest
nº	número	number
O	Oeste	West
º	grau(s)	degrees
Pç.	Praça	Plaza
P.S.*	Post Scriptum	Post Script
P.S.P.*	Polícia de Segurança Pública	Public Safety Organization
pág.	página	page
PJ	Polícia Judiciária	(criminal) police
R.	Rua	Street
S	Sul	South
SE	Sudeste	Southeast
séc.	século	century
SO	Sudoeste	Southwest
Sta./Sto.	Santa/Santo	Saint
tel.	telefone	phone number

3.9.2 Abbreviations of weights and measures

cm	centímetros	centimeters
cm^2	centímetros quadrados	square centimeters
cm^3	centímetros cúbicos	cubic centimeters
gr.	grama	gram
h.	hora	hour
hec.	hectares	hectares
kg.	quilograma	kilogram
km/h	quilómetros por hora	kilometers per/hour
kw.	quilowatts	kilowatts
l	litros	liters
m	metros	meters
m^2	metros quadrados	square meters
m^3	metros cúbicos	cubic meters
mm	milímetros	milimeters

3.9.3   National and international organizations

BM*	Banco Mundial (World Bank)
CD*	Corpo Diplomático (Diplomatic Corps)
CDS* (Pt)	Centro Democrático Social
CE*	Comunidade Europeia (EC)
CGTP*	Confederação Geral dos Trabalhadores Portugueses
CGTP-IN*	Confederação Geral dos Trabalhadores Portugueses-Intersindical Nacional
CML*	Câmara Municipal de Lisboa
CPLP*	Comunidade dos Países de Língua Portuguesa
EUA*	Estados Unidos da América (USA)
FMI*	Fundo Monetário Internacional (IMF)
FNLA*	Frente Nacional de Libertação de Angola
FRELIMO	Frente de Libertação de Moçambique
FRETILIN	Frente Revolucionária de Timor-Leste Independente
MERCOSUL	Mercado dos Países do Sul (economic union consisting of Brazil, Uruguay, Paraguay, and Argentina)
MPLA*	Movimento Popular da Libertação de Angola
NATO	Organização do Tratado do Atlântico Norte (NATO)
OLP*	Organização de Libertação da Palestina (PLO)
ONU	Organização das Nações Unidas (UNO)
OPEP	Organização dos Países Exportadores de Petróleo (OPEC)
PAIGC*	Partido Africano da Independência da Guiné e Cabo Verde
PALOP	Países Africanos de Língua Oficial Portuguesa
PCB*	Partido Comunista Brasileiro
PCBR*	Partido Comunista Brasileiro Revolucionário
PCP*	Partido Comunista Português
PDG*	Partido Democrático da Guiné
PESODUMO	Partido Socialista Democrata Unido de Moçambique
PEV*	Partido Ecológico "Os Verdes"
PI* (Br)	Partido Integralista
PIB*	Produto Interno Bruto
PIDE	Polícia Internacional de Defesa do Estado
PM* (Br)	Polícia Militar

PNB*	Produto Nacional Bruto
PP* (Pt)	Partido Popular
PPB*	Partido Progressista Brasileiro
PPM* (Pt)	Partido Popular Monárquico
PS* (Br) (Pt)	Partido Socialista
PSD* (Pt)	Partido Social Democrata
PT* (Br)	Partido Trabalhista
RDP*	Rádio Difusão Portuguesa
RENAMO	Resistência Nacional Moçambicana
RFA*	República Federal Alemã
RGA*	Reunião Geral de Alunos
RTP*	Rádio Televisão Portuguesa
SA*	Sociedade Anónima (Inc.)
SIC	Sociedade Independente de Comunicação
UNITA	União Nacional para a Independência Total de Angola

3.10   Numerals

The chief difference in the written representation of numbers in Portuguese is the use of the period to show separation between hundreds, thousands, millions, etc., and the use of a comma instead of a decimal point. Numbers are generally written out as words in letters and documents, whereas years and dates are presented in digit form. While tens and ones are separated by a hyphen in English, they are separated by *e* (and) in Portuguese. Hundreds and tens are also separated by *e*.

Examples:
Comprei vinte e cinco galinhas no mercado.
I bought twenty-five chickens at the market.
Nasceu no ano 1924.
He was born in the year 1924.

Years are pronounced as complete numbers in Portuguese so that 1924 is pronounced "mil novecentos e vinte e quatro."

Centuries are always written with Roman numerals: "Século xx" – twentieth century.

3.10.1   Cardinal and ordinal numbers

1	um (f uma)	primeiro
2	dois (f duas)	segundo
3	três	terceiro
4	quatro	quarto
5	cinco	quinto
6	seis	sexto
7	sete	sétimo
8	oito	oitavo
9	nove	nono
10	dez	décimo
11	onze	décimo primeiro
12	doze	décimo segundo
13	treze	décimo terceiro
14	catorze	décimo quarto
15	quinze	décimo quinto
16	dezesseis, dezasseis	décimo sexto
17	dezessete, dezassete	décimo sétimo
18	dezoito	décimo oitavo
19	dezenove, dezanove	décimo nono
20	vinte	vigésimo
21	vinte e um	vigésimo primeiro
30	trinta	trigésimo
40	quarenta	quadragésimo
50	cinquenta	quinquagésimo
60	sessenta	sexagésimo
70	setenta	septuagésimo
80	oitenta	octogésimo
90	noventa	nonagésimo
100	cem	centésimo
101	cento e um	centésimo primeiro
200	duzentos	ducentésimo
300	trezentos	trecentésimo
400	quatrocentos	quadringentésimo
500	quinhentos	quingentésimo
600	seiscentos	seiscentésimo, sexcentésimo
700	setecentos	septingentésimo
800	oitocentos	octingentésimo
900	novecentos	nongentésimo
1.000	mil	milésimo
2.000	dois mil	dumilésimo

Some of the cardinal numbers also must agree in gender with the nouns they modify:

1 – um carro, uma casa
2 – dois carros, duas casas
Also all numbers ending in a hundred except for 100.

200 – duzentos carros, duzentas casas

All of the ordinal numbers are adjectives and therefore agree with their nouns in gender and number. When written, the ordinal numbers can be presented with the number plus the terminations *–o, -a, -os, -as* in superscript and underlined.

Examples:
56ª Reunião Anual dos Autores Nacionais
56th Annual Meeting of National Authors.

The larger numbers differ from English:
1.000.000 – um milhão
1.000.000.000 – mil milhões
1.000.000.000.000 – um bilhão

3.11 Measurements

3.11.1 Currencies

Angola	kwanza (m)
Brazil	real, reais (m)
Cape Verde	escudo (m)
Guinea Bissau	peso (m)
Moçambique	metical, meticais (m)
Portugal	euro (formerly: escudo) (m)
São Tomé and Príncipe	dobra (f)
United Kingdom	libra (f)
United States	dólar(es) (m)

3.11.2 Dates

In Portuguese, the date is always given in the following order: date, month, year.

Orally the date would be given thus:
Hoje são quinze de junho de mil novecentos e noventa e cinco.
Today is June 15, nineteen ninety-five.

In written discourse the date is presented in the following manner, with the day and year given in numerals:

A guerra acabou dia 2 de Janeiro de 1935.
The war ended on January 2, 1935.

In letter headings, the date may be given simply with numbers, starting with the day. The day, month, and year are separated by a hyphen or slash.

Example:
2-3-67 is March 2, 1967.

In letters the month may also be written out:

Example:
2 de Março, 1967

3.11.2.1 Months and days of the week

Months are capitalized in Portugal and Africa but not in Brazil. Days are not capitalized in Portuguese.

Months

Janeiro	January
Fevereiro	February
Março	March
Abril	April
Maio	May
Junho	June
Julho	July
Agosto	August
Setembro	September
Outubro	October
Novembro	November
Dezembro	December

Days

domingo	Sunday
segunda-feira	Monday
terça-feira	Tuesday
quarta-feira	Wednesday
quinta-feira	Thursday
sexta-feira	Friday
sábado	Saturday

The ending *–feira* can be omitted. Week days can be abbreviated in written informal discourse: 2^a, 3^a, 4^a, 5^a, 6^a.

3.11.3 Time

Time in Portuguese is represented as in English when written but instead of "am" and "pm" one uses *da manhã* (in the morning), *da tarde* (in the afternoon), *da noite* (at night). *Da madrugada* may occasionally be heard to indicate early morning (before sunrise).

There are several ways of telling the time in Portuguese.

Basic manner of asking the time:
—Que horas são?(Pt) /Que horas você tem? (Br)

In telling time, one o'clock and any time relating to one o'clock takes the singular form of *ser* while any other time is given by the plural form of this verb. The feminine forms of 1 and 2 (*uma* and *duas*) are used for the hour.

Examples:
1:12 pm
É uma e doze da tarde.
It is one twelve in the afternoon.

12:40 pm
É uma menos vinte da tarde.
It is twenty to one in the afternoon.

After the half hour, the time may be told either referring to the next hour or the last so that 12:40 may also be stated as *são doze e quarenta* (it is twelve forty).

2:17 pm
São duas e dezessete da tarde.
It is two seventeen in the afternoon.

The twenty-four hour clock is used for official times (train schedules etc.).

The following expressions are also used to tell time:
meia-noite (midnight)
Faltam vinte minutos para a meia-noite.
It is twenty to midnight.
(*meia-noite* is a feminine word)

meio-dia (noon)
São dez para o meio-dia.
It is ten to twelve.
(*meio-dia* is a masculine word)

um quarto (quarter hour)
São três e um quarto.
It is a quarter past three.

meia (half hour)
> **São seis e meia.**
> It is half past six.

em ponto (sharp)
> **Então encontramo-nos às cinco em ponto.**
> We'll meet at 5 sharp then.

atrasado (late)
> **Cheguei atrasado ao jantar.**
> I arrived late to the dinner.

adiantado (early)
> **Não conheço ninguém que chegue adiantado.**
> I don't know anyone who arrives early.

a horas (on time)
> **Não gosto de chegar nem atrasada nem adiantada, mas a horas.**
> I don't like to arrive early or late, but on time.

a tempo (in time)
> **Quase não chegavam a tempo de apanhar o comboio.** (Pt)
> They barely arrived in time to catch the train.

3.11.4 Weight

The verb *pesar* is used to express weight, followed by a metric weight unit.

Example:
Peso 160 quilos.
I weigh 160 kilos.

Weight can also be used to designate a quantity.

Example:
Comprei dois quilos de morangos.
I bought two kilos of strawberries.

Note: All weight units are masculine, including *grama*, except for *tonelada*.

---

uma tonelada
um quilo, dez quilos
um grama, duzentos gramas
um decigrama
um miligrama
um micrograma

3.11.5 Distance

All Lusophone countries use the metric system. Units for length, and therefore distance, are the following in Portuguese:

metros (meters)
quilómetros (kilometers)

Non–metric terms:

passos (steps)
degraus (stair steps)

The words for English measurements are:

um pé (foot)
uma milha (mile)
uma polegada (inch)

In order to express distances with units of measurement, use *ficar* + *a* or *ser* + *a*.

Examples:
A estação fica a 5 quilómetros daqui.
The station is five kilometers from here.

Sintra é a 30 quilómetros de Lisboa.
Sintra is 30 kilometers from Lisbon.

In order to express distances without units (i.e. far from, or near) use *ficar* or *ser*.
Some terms include:
longe (far away)
longe de (far from)
perto (close by)
perto de (close to)
entre (between)
para além de (beyond)
antes de (before)
depois de (after)

Examples:
A minha casa fica na Rua das Cruzes para além do cinema novo.
My house is on Cruzes Road beyond the new movie theater.

Vamos ao restaurante brasileiro, é aqui perto.
Let's go to the Brazilian restaurant, it's close by.

3.11.6 Temperatures

All Portuguese-speaking countries use centigrades to express temperature.
The word *graus* means "degrees."

The temperature in Portuguese is expressed in the following ways:

Estar + temperature
Estão 24 graus. It [the temperature] is 24 degrees.

A temperatura é de + temperature
A temperatura máxima é de 42 graus. The maximum temperature is 42 degrees.

3.11.7 Sizes

The verb *medir* is used to express height or length, followed by a metric weight unit. Note that *medir* is irregular in the first person singular of the present indicative.

Example:
— **Quanto mede?**	How tall are you?
—**Meço um metro e setenta (cm)**.	I'm 1 meter 70 tall.

Other vocabulary related to sizes:
For people: **baixo** (short), **alto** (tall).

Sizes of clothes, shoes and other objects can be expressed in different manners, either by exact numbers or in general categories such as small, medium, and large. It is suggested, since standards differ throughout the Lusophone world, that visitors always try on clothing and do not just depend on size indicators.

For clothes:

apertado	tight
comprido	long
curto	short
devolver o dinheiro	to return the money
experimentar	to try on
fica bem	it looks good
grande	large
largo	large, big
número	size
número acima, número abaixo	one size up/down
pequeno	small
que número calça(s)/veste(s)?	what size do you wear?
reclamação, reclamar	a/to return; to complain, complaint
trocar	to exchange

3.11.8   Quantities

The following terms are used to denote special quantities.

alguns	some, a few
década	decade
dezena	a quantity of ten
dúzia	dozen
imensos	a great quantity of
muito/a/os/as	many, a lot of
quarteirão	twenty-five (a "quarter")
uma mão-cheia	a handful
um ramo	a bunch (of flowers)
vários	several

3.12   Interjections

3.12.1   Religious

Com os diabos! (Damn!, Devil take it!)
Deus nos/me valha/acuda! (God help us/me!)
Meu Deus! (My God!)
Nossa Senhora!, Minha Nossa Senhora! (Our Lady!)
Ó Céus! (Heavens!)
Ó Diabo! (Damn!)
Raios me partam! (Damn it!, literally "let thunderbolts split me!")
   (Pt)
Santo Deus! (Holy God!)

3.12.2   Pain

Au!, Ui! (Ouch!)

3.12.3   Surprise

A sério?! (Seriously?)
Ah!
Caramba! (Wow!)
Hã?! (the equivalent of "huh?" or "um?")
Não me diga(s)! (You don't say!)
O quê?! (What?!)

3.12.4 Rage

All terms which are extremely vulgar or profane are marked by an asterisk.

These are applied to a person:

Cabra!* (f) (Pt) (Bitch!)
Cabrão!* (m) (Pt) (Asshole!)
Cabrona!* (f) (Pt) (Asshole! / Bitch!)
Cadela!* (f) (Bitch! / Whore!)
Filho da puta!* (m) (Son of a bitch!)
Filha da puta!* (f) (Bitch!)
Foda-se!* (Pt) (Fuck you!)
Idiota! Imbecil! (These are the least offensive and correspond to "You idiot!")
Puta!* (f) (Whore! / Bitch!)
Vai-te foder!* (Pt) (Fuck you!)
Vagabunda!* (f) (Br) (Whore!)
Vagabundo!* (m) (Br) (Piece of shit!)
Vai apanhar no cu!* (Shove it up your ass!)
Veado!* (Br) (Pejorative term for homosexuals)
Bicha!* (Br) (Pejorative term for homosexuals)

These are used in general situations:

Caralho!* (Pt) (Fuck!)
Merda!* (Shit!)
Pomba!* (Br) (Fuck!)

3.12.5 Joy

Fabuloso! (Fabulous!)
Fantástico! (Fantastic!)
Magnífico! (Magnificent!)
Parabéns! (similar to "Congratulations!")
Que beleza! (Br) (Wonderful!)

3.12.6 Warning

Atenção! (Look out!)
Cuidado! (Careful!)

3.12.7 Pity

Coitado/a! (You poor thing!)
Pobre diabo! (This expression is used to talk about a man, and not to the person. Poor devil!)

3.13 Collective nouns

uma alcateia	a pack of wolves
um bando	a flock of birds
um bando de ladrões	a band of thieves
uma cáfila	a herd of camels
um canavial	a bamboo forest
um cardume	a school of fish
um engenho	a farm for sugar production (with the machinery)
um enxame	a swarm of bees
um gangue	a gang
uma junta	a team of oxen
um laranjal	an orange grove
uma manada	a herd of cattle
uma matilha	a pack of dogs
uma ninhada	a group of baby animals
um olival	an olive grove
um pinhal	a pine forest
um pomar	a grove (in general)
um rebanho	a herd of sheep
uma récua	a group of beasts of burden
um souto	a chestnut grove
uma turma	a class (such as a group of students at the same level); a group of friends. (Br)
uma vara	a group of pigs
uma vinha	a vineyard

3.14 Animal sounds

Animal	Verb
abelha–bee	**zumbir, zumbar**
burro–donkey, burro	**zurrar**
camelo–camel	**blaterar**

121

cão/cachorro-dog	ladrar, latir (bark), ganir (whine), uivar (howl)
gato-cat	miar
cavalo-horse	relinchar
corvo-crow	crocitar
galinha-hen	cacarejar
galo-rooster	cantar
leão-lion	rugir
macaco-monkey	guinchar
ovelha-sheep	balir
papagaio-parrot	palrar
pássaro-bird	cantar (sing), piar (chirp, peep as in chicks)
pato-duck	grasnar
peru-turkey	grugulejar
pombo-dove, pigeon	arrulhar
porco-pig	grunhir (grunt)
rã-frog	coaxar
rato-mouse	chiar
serpente-snake	assobiar
vaca-cow	mugir

3.15   Onomatopeic words

bramir	to roar (as in a beast or the ocean)
chapinhar	to splash
chiar	to squeak (as in a mouse or a door)
cochichar	to speak in a low voice (has a negative connotation)
ding-dong	ding-dong
o frufru	rustle (noun)
gaguejar	to stutter
gargarejar	to gargle
guinchar	to squeal
pipilar	to chirp
pum!	boom!
ranger	to squeak
ribombar	to thunder
roncar	to snore
ronronar	to purr
sibilar	to whiz (as in a bullet)

sussurar	to whisper
tique–taque	tick tock
troar	to thunder
um silvo	the sound of a ship's or train's whistle
zás-trás	the sound of a slap

3.16 Terms of courtesy

The following are terms and expressions used to express thanks, ask for favors, and beg pardon. The conditional form may also be used to express politeness and this use is being taken over by the indicative *pretérito imperfeito* in contemporary usage.

Com licença	Excuse me. To be used when walking in front of someone or when asking to be excused from a table, meeting, etc.
	Examples:
	"Com licença," disse António tentando passar entre várias pessoas.
	"Excuse me," said Antonio, trying to pass through the group of people.
	"Com licença," disse o deputado para pedir a palavra.
	"Excuse me," said the congressman when asking leave to speak.
	Quando jantávamos em casa dos meus avós, tínhamos de pedir sempre licença antes de nos levantarmos.
	When we used to eat at my grandparents', we always had to ask for permission before leaving the table.
Perdão	Excuse me, I'm sorry. To be used when approaching someone to ask a direction, to correct oneself, etc.
	Example:
	Perdão mas estão chamando a Senhora Diretora no telefone. (Br)
	Excuse me, you have a call.

Desculpe	The same as *perdão* but less formal.
	Example:
	Desculpe, sabe dizer-me onde fica o Ministério da Educação?
	Excuse me, can you tell me where the Ministry of Education is?
Desculpa	The same as *desculpe* but the least formal due to the informal form of address *tu*.
	Example:
	Desculpa, não queria magoar-te/te magoar.
	I'm sorry, I did not mean to hurt you.
Se faz favor	The same as *por favor*. If enunciated very fast, becomes "sefachfavor." (Pt)
	Example:
	Uma cerveja, se faz favor.
	A beer, please.
Por favor	Please.
	Example:
	Pode tomar nota dum recado, por favor?
	Could you take a message please?
Pois não?	Yes [may I help you]?: opens a dialogue where a service is implied, e.g. waiting at a table, helping a customer, etc. Only used in Brazil.
	Example:
	Pois não, a senhora deseja alguma coisa?
	Hello, what would you like to order?
	Sim, podia me trazer um suco de abacaxi e um sanduiche de queijo?
	Yes, I'd like a pineapple juice and a cheese sandwich, please.
Obrigado/a	Thank you. The ending agrees with the speaker's gender.
	Example:
	"Obrigada," disse Júlia quando recebeu o presente.
	"Thank you," said Julia upon receiving the gift.

De nada.	You're welcome.
	Example:
	"De nada," respondi quando ela me agradeceu.
	"You're welcome," I said when she thanked me.
Fazer o obséquio de . . .	To request a favor. This is very formal.
	Example:
	Fazia-me o obséquio de chamar o Director? (Pt)
	Could you do me a favor and call the manager?
Posso . . .?	May I?
	Example:
	Posso entrar?
	May I come in?
Desejava . . .	I wish to . . . , I would like to . . .
	Example:
	Desejava enviar esta encomenda por correio aéreo.
	I wish to send this package by air mail.
Queria . . .	Same as *desejava*.
	Example:
	Queria 250 gr. de fiambre.
	I would like 250 grams of ham.

4 Nouns and adjectives

4.1 Nouns and gender

Portuguese nouns all belong to one of two genders. All nouns which may combine with the article *o* are generally considered masculine, while all nouns which may combine with the article *a* are generally considered feminine. The noun decides the form for all adjectives which are used as its modifiers in both gender and number.

The gender of most Portuguese nouns can be easily identified by the ending. Words ending in –*o* are almost always masculine while words ending in –*a* are almost always feminine:

o carro (car)	**a cadeira** (chair)
o livro (book)	**a mesa** (table)
o sapato (shoe)	**a casa** (house)
o relógio (clock)	**a justiça** (justice)
o deserto (desert)	**a caneta** (pen)
o conceito (concept)	**a loucura** (insanity)

Most words ending in –*ade* are feminine:

a realidade (reality)
a verdade (the truth)
a mocidade (youth)
a velocidade (velocity)
a idade (age)
a vaidade (vanity)

Words ending in –*or* are generally masculine. In the case of words referring to professions, in order to show that the noun refers to a woman, an –*a* is added:

um jogador (male athlete or player)	**uma jogadora** (female athlete or player)
um cantor (male singer)	**uma cantora** (female singer)

Most words ending in *–ção* are feminine:

---

a condição (condition)
a tentação (temptation)
a perdição (perdition)
a salvação (salvation)
a maldição (curse)
a putrefacção (putrefaction)
a jurisdição (jurisdiction)

However, there are several exceptions to this general rule: *o coração* (heart), *o leão* (lion), *o cão* (dog [Pt]), *o pão* (bread), *o caldeirão* (a big, or communal, cooking pot), *o bastão* (stick). Often, the augmentatives of feminine words become masculine: *o portão* (entrance, big door or gate, from *a porta*, door); *o mulherão* (big woman, from *a mulher*, woman).

Most words ending in *–em* are feminine:

---

uma viagem (a trip or voyage)
uma passagem (a passage)
uma paisagem (a landscape)
uma mensagem (a message)

Exceptions include: *o homem* (man) and *o lobisomem* (werewolf)

Most words of Greek origin ending in *–ama*, *-ema*, and *–oma* are masculine despite ending in *–a* in Portuguese:

---

o grama (gram)
o telegrama (telegram)
o fonema (phoneme)
o estratagema (scheme)
o anátema (curse)
o coma (comma)
o axioma (axiom)
o problema (problem)

Some words are masculine and end in *–a* for the reason that historically they were (and mostly still are!) reserved exclusively for men:

---

o pirata (pirate – with a few exceptions!)
o papa (the pope)
o jesuíta (the jesuit)
o patriarca (patriarch)
o papá (father)

Some words ending in –*a* or –*o* may be either masculine or feminine depending upon whether the person referred to is male or female:

o modelo (male model)	**a modelo** (female model)
o artista (male artist)	**a artista** (female artist)

Other words following this pattern include:

o/a acrobata (acrobat)
o/a camarada (comrade)
o/a colega (colleague)
o/a compatriota (compatriot)
o/a dentista (dentist)
o/a homicida (murderer)
o/a indígena (indigenous person)
o/a infanticida (murderer of children)
o/a jornalista (journalist)
o/a pianista (pianist)
o/a patriota (patriot)
o/a suicida (person who commits suicide)
o/a violinista (violinist)

Words ending in –*e* generally do not follow any rule with regard to gender, and their gender must be sought in a dictionary.

The following words ending in –*nte* follow same pattern as the words in the previous group for masculine and feminine forms:

o/a gerente (manager)
o/a agente (agent)
o/a estudante (student)
o/a cliente (client)
o/a servente (servant)
o/a imigrante (immigrant)

Words with other endings which also follow this pattern include:

o/a herege (heretic)
o/a mártir (martyr)
o/a colegial (student in a private school)
o/a intérprete (interpreter)
o/a hóspede (guest)
o/a presidente (president)
o/a jovem (a youth)

Some words ending in *–e* change their ending to *–a* when referring to females:

o **mestre** (male teacher)	a **mestra** (female teacher)
o **monge** (monk)	a **monja** (nun)
o **infante** (son of the royal family)	a **infanta** (daughter of the royal family)

Some words have different forms when referring to women or men:

uma **avó** (a grandmother)	um **avô** (a grandfather)
uma **baronesa** (a baroness)	um **barão** (a baron)
uma **condessa** (a countess)	um **conde** (a count)
uma **czarina** (a czarina)	um **czar** (a czar)
uma **duquesa** (a duchess)	um **duque** (a duke)
uma **embaixatriz** (a female ambassador)	um **embaixador** (an ambassador)
uma **freira** (a nun)	um **frade** (a friar)
uma **heroína** (a heroine or female hero)	um **herói** (a male hero)
uma **jogralesa** (a female troubador)	um **jogral** (a male troubador)
uma **marquesa** (a marquise)	um **marquês** (a marquis)
uma **poetisa*** (a female poet)	um **poeta** (a male poet)
uma **princesa** (a princess)	um **príncipe** (a prince)
uma **profetisa*** (a female prophet)	um **profeta** (a male prophet)
uma **rainha** (queen)	um **rei** (a king)
uma **rapariga** (a girl or young woman, Pt)	um **rapaz** (a boy or young man)
uma **ré** (a female defendant)	um **réu** (a male defendant)
uma **sacerdotisa** (a priestess)	um **sacerdote** (a priest)

*In these cases, in current usage it is common to use the same (masculine) form in order to avoid sexist speech.

4.2 Number

4.2.1 General rule

The rules for pluralizing nouns also apply to adjectives.

In Portuguese as in English, the plurals of nouns are generally formed by adding *–s* if the word ends in a vowel and *–es* if the word ends in a consonant (*-r*, *-z*, or *-n*):

a casa (the house)	as casas
o jogador (the player)	os jogadores
o cânone (the literary canon)	os cânones
a raiz (the root)	as raízes
o rapaz (the boy)	os rapazes

For words ending in –*m*, the final *m* is replaced by –*n* before adding the plural –*s*:

o homem (the man)	os homens
a vagem (the pod)	as vagens

Words ending in an unstressed vowel + *s* do not change in the plural:

o lápis (the pencil)	os lápis
o ônibus (Br) (the bus)	os ônibus

4.2.2 Words ending in -*l*

For words ending in –*al*, -*el*, -*ol*, and –*ul*, the final -*l* is replaced by -*i* before adding the mark of the plural, –*s*. The plurals of words ending in –*ol* and –*el* have a written accent on that syllable.

o animal (the animal)	os animais
o azul (the blue)	os azuis
o casal (the couple)	os casais
o espanhol (the Spaniard)	os espanhóis
o hotel (the hotel)	os hotéis
o lençol (the sheet)	os lençóis
o papel (the paper)	os papéis
o paul (the swamp)	os pauis

Exceptions include: **mal–males, cônsul–cônsules.**

For words ending in unstressed –*il*, the final -*il* is replaced by –*eis*.

If the word ends in stressed –*il*, then the -*l* is replaced by -*s*.

o fóssil (the fossil)	os fósseis
o réptil (the reptile)	os répteis
o barril (the barrel)	os barris
o fuzil (the rifle)	os fuzis

4.2.3 Words ending in -ão

The general rule for pluralizing words ending in –ão is to replace the ending with –õe before adding the final –s.

a invenção (the invention)	as invenções
a limitação (the limitation)	as limitações
o casarão (the mansion)	os casarões
o coração (the heart)	os corações
o limão (the lemon)	os limões

There are some words ending in –ão whose plural forms end in –ães.

Example:

o alemão – os alemães (the German man – the German men)

o bastião (the bastion)
o cão (the dog)
o catalão (the Catalan)
o capitão (the capitan)
o capelão (the chaplain)
o charlatão (the charlatan)
o escrivão (the scribe)
o guardião (the guardian)
o pão (the bread)
o sacristão (the sacristan)
o tabelião (the notary)

The following words ending in –ão form the plural by simply adding a final –s.

Example: irmão – irmãos (brother – brothers)

a benção (the blessing)
o acordão (the agreement)
o cidadão (the citizen)
o cortesão (the courtesan)
o cristão (the Christian)
o desvão (the hiding place, garret)
o órfão (the orphan)
o órgão (the organ)
o pagão (the pagan)
o sótão (the attic)

4.2.4 Words with only plural forms

The following words exist only in their plural forms:

---

as **alvíssaras** (finder's reward; the tidings)
as **belas-artes** (the fine arts)
as **calendas** (the kalends – the first day of the month in the Roman calendar)
as **cãs** (the grey hairs)
as **condolências** (the condolences)
as **exéquias** (the funeral rites)
as **férias** (the vacation)
as **fezes** (the feces)
as **matinas** (the morning prayers)
as **núpcias** (the wedding celebration, the nuptials)
as **olheiras** (the bags under the eyes)
as **primícias** (the first fruits)
os **anais** (the annals)
os **antolhos** (Pt) (the blinders, blinkers, eyeshade)
os **arredores** (the surroundings)
os **esponsais** (the betrothment, engagement)
os **óculos** (the eyeglasses)
os **pêsames** (sympathy wishes regarding a death)
os **víveres** (reserve of food)

The four suits of cards are also always referred to in the plural:

---

as **copas** (hearts)
as **espadas** (spades)
os **ouros** (diamonds)
os **paus** (clubs)

4.3 Word order

4.3.1 Sentence structure

Subjects generally precede the verb in both questions and statements.

Note: The subject pronoun in Portuguese can always be omitted if it is obvious from the context or the verb form:

Examples:
Falo português.
I speak Portuguese.

Você quer ir almoçar?
Do you want to eat lunch?

Adverbs of negation usually come between the subject and the verb:

Example:
Ela não quer ir.
She does not want to go.

4.3.2 Nouns and their modifiers

- Articles always precede the noun.
  Example:
  Tenho um carro.
  I have a car.

- Articles and demonstrative, possessive, and indefinite adjectives always precede the noun.
  Examples:
  O escritório está vazio.
  The office is empty.

  Este livro é interessante.
  This book is interesting.

  O meu tio é um pintor famoso.
  My uncle is a famous painter.

  Algumas pessoas ficaram doentes depois do jantar.
  Some people were sick after the dinner.

- Indefinite adjectives which show negation generally precede the noun, but may follow it, especially if the noun is not modified by other adjectives and is at the end of a sentence.
  Examples:
  Não há nenhum restaurante português na minha cidade.
  There are no Portuguese restaurants in my city.

  Não há problema nenhum.
  It's no problem.

- Numbers always precede the noun that they modify.
  Example:
  Visitei dois países de língua portuguesa no Verão.
  I visited two Portuguese-speaking countries over the summer.

- Nationalities always follow the noun they modify.
  Example:
  Uma família italiana.
  An Italian family.

- Non-quantitative adjectives generally follow the noun but can also follow the verb.

Examples:
A casa é grande.
The house is big.

A casa nova do Luís é grande.
Luís's new house is big.

- Certain adjectives have different meanings depending on whether they occur before or after the noun they modify. When the adjective comes in its regular position, i.e. after the noun, it denotes a literal meaning, whereas before the verb it acquires a figurative meaning.

Examples:
Comprei um carro novo.
I bought a brand new car.

Comprei um novo carro.
I bought a new/another car (it's only new to me).

Note: Adjectives may also precede the noun when for purposes of emphasis the speaker wishes to stress its uniqueness. In this case the adjective functions as an epithet.

Examples:
O conhecido escritor daquela cidade entrou como actor no filme.
The famous writer from that town starred in the movie. (In this case "famous writer" is actually used as one term.)

O escritor famoso daquela cidade entrou como actor no filme.
The writer who is famous from that town starred in the movie.
(The town may have other writers but they are not famous.)

4.4   Adjectives

Adjectives in Portuguese agree in number and gender with the noun that they modify. The rules for the formation of plural and feminine forms are the same as those for nouns (see Sections 4.1 and 4.2).

Gosto de gatos pretos.
I like black cats.

4.4.1   Adjectives with different meaning depending on position

The following adjectives have different meanings depending on whether they precede or follow the noun. If they follow the noun,

the meaning is literal, and if they precede the noun, they are
figurative.

alto	**Eu vivo num prédio muito alto.** I live in a very tall building. **Os altos dignatários de várias nações reuniram-se em Praga.** The high (important) dignitaries of several nations met in Prague.
antigo	**Aquele carro antigo vale muito dinheiro.** That old (antique) car is worth a lot of money. **O meu antigo carro era preto.** My old (former) car was black.
grande	**Comprei uma casa grande.** I bought a big house. **Fernando Pessoa é um grande poeta.** Fernando Pessoa is a great poet.
novo	**Tenho uma nova namorada.** I have a new girlfriend. **Tenho uma namorada nova.** I have a young girlfriend. (In colloquial speech this sentence may mean the same as the previous one.)
pobre	**As famílias pobres receberam um subsídio do governo.** The poor families received money from the government. **O pobre homem ainda está no hospital.** The poor (showing pity) man is still in the hospital.
simples	**Embora fosse muito rico, era um homem simples.** Although he was rich, he was a very simple man (unpretentious). **Ele era um simples empregado do estado.** He was a mere government employee.
velho	**Joguei fora meus sapatos velhos.** (Br) I threw out my old shoes. **O meu velho amigo veio me visitar.** My old (long time) friend came to visit me.

4.4.2 Demonstrative adjectives

For demonstrative adjectives see Section 7.2.6.

4.4.3 Possessive adjectives

The possessive adjectives in Portuguese agree with the possessor in number and person and with the object possessed in number and gender. The formation of plural forms is the same as that for nouns. In Portugal the possessives are usually preceded by the definite article, but in Brazil they sometimes are not.

Note: The possessive pronouns share the same form as the adjectives but always require the definite article, and the object is omitted.

The forms are the following:

meu(s), minha(s)	my
teu(s), tua(s)	your (singular, informal)
seu(s), sua(s)	his, her, its, your (formal) (Pt); your (informal) (Br)
dele, dela	his, her, its (unambiguous form)
nosso(s), nossa(s)	our
vosso(s), vossa(s) (Pt)	your (pl) (Pt)
seu(s), sua(s)	your (formal) (Pt); your (informal) (Br)
deles, delas	their (unambiguous)
seu(s), sua(s)	their

Note: *Vosso* and *vossa* are not used in Brazil; in Portugal, *seu(s)*, *sua(s)* is more formal than the former for "your" (pl).

Examples:
Gosto muito dos seus sapatos novos, Sra. Noémia. (Pt)
I like your new shoes very much, Ms. Noémia.

Gosto muito de seus sapatos novos, Dulce. (Br)
Gosto muito de teus sapatos novos, Dulce. (This implies closeness, or a very informal relationship.)

(A) nossa mãe está muito contente.
Our mother is very happy.

Tenho o bilhete dele, mas não tenho o meu.
I have his ticket but I don't have mine.

5 Verbs

Portuguese verbs fall into three groups based upon their infinitive endings. These are *–ar*, *-er*, and *–ir*. There are six verbal inflexions which correspond to seven personal pronouns: *eu*, *tu*, *você* (which shares the same inflexion as *ele/ela*), *nós*, *vós*, and *vocês* (which shares the forms with *eles/elas*). The *vós* form is now archaic. In most regions of Brazil, *você* is usually used instead of *tu*, which is standard in Portugal and Lusophone Africa.

5.1 Simple indicative mode tenses

The indicative mode in Portuguese is used for main clauses and subordinate clauses after many expressions.

5.1.1 Present tense

The present tense (*Presente do Indicativo*) is used to express actions in the present, thoughts, opinions, physical and mental states, and descriptions.

The conjugations for regular verbs in the present are given here to give a basic idea of the Portuguese verb system. There are many irregular verbs in the present whose forms are given in conjugation manuals.

	-ar **falar (to speak)**	*-er* **comer (to eat)**	*-ir* **resumir (to summarize)**
eu (I)	falo	como	resumo
tu (you)	falas	comes	resumes
você (you) ele (he) ela (she)	fala	come	resume
nós (we)	falamos	comemos	resumimos
vocês (you), eles (they-m) elas (they-f)	falam	comem	resumem

Examples:
Acho que tu precisas de ter mais cuidado. (Pt)
I think that you need to be more careful.

Os convidados chegam hoje.
The guests arrive today.

Note 1: The present can also be used to express an idea in the future, or a customary action in the present.

Examples:
Faço as compras amanhã.
I'll go shopping tomorrow.

Eles têm sempre aulas de manhã.
They always have classes in the morning.

Note 2: Many verbs in Portuguese have an irregular stem in the present, often in the first person singular.

Examples:

dar:	dou
dizer:	digo
dormir:	durmo
estar:	estou
fazer:	faço
ir:	vou
ouvir:	ouço
pedir:	peço
perder:	perco
poder:	posso
pôr:	ponho
seguir:	sigo
sentir:	sinto
ser:	sou
ter:	tenho
trazer:	trago
ver:	vejo
vir:	venho

5.1.2 Preterit tense

The preterit tense (*Pretérito Perfeito*) is used to express the beginning or/and the end of an action in the past.

The following chart shows the endings to be added to the stem of the infinitive. There are many irregular verbs in the preterit which can be found in conjugation manuals.

	-ar	*-er*	*-ir*
eu	-ei	–i	-i
tu	(a)ste	(e)ste	(i)ste
você, ele, ela	-ou	(e)u	(i)u
nós	(á)mos (Pt)	(e)mos	(i)mos
	(a)mos (Br)		
vocês, eles, elas	(a)ram	(e)ram	(i)ram

Examples:

Liguei para casa dos meus pais ontem.
I called my parents' house yesterday (the action was completed).

Soube desse problema quando ele o comentou comigo.
I found out about that problem when he told me about it. (This begins with the verb *saber* [to know], and ends with the verb *comentar* [to tell]).

Consegui abrir a janela com a ajuda deles.
I managed to open the window with their help.

Fui a Moçambique uma vez.
I went to Mozambique once.

Note: The preterite tense is used with "never" and "ever" or "any time."

Nunca fui a São Tomé e Príncipe.
I never went to São Tomé and Principe.

5.1.3   Imperfect tense

Another past tense in Portuguese is the imperfect (*Pretérito Imperfeito*). The following chart shows the endings to be added to the stem of the infinitive.

	-ar	*-er*	*-ir*
eu	-ava	-ia	-ia
tu	-avas	-ias	-ias
você, ele, ela	- ava	-ia	-ia
nós	-ávamos	-íamos	-íamos
vocês, eles, elas	-avam	-iam	-iam

Note: the *nós* form always takes an accent as shown above.
Some verbs are irregular in the *Imperfeito*. Their forms are the following:

---

pôr (to put): eu punha, tu punhas, você punha, etc.
ser (to be): eu era, tu eras, você era, etc.
ter (to have): eu tinha, tu tinhas, você tinha, etc.
vir (to come): eu vinha, tu vinhas, você vinha, etc.

The imperfect is used to express any other point of an action in the past (not the beginning or end). Some typical examples of its use are to express:

* descriptions
* physical and mental states (as it is difficult to know when they begin or end)
* clock time
* age (when not expressing birthdays, i.e. the beginning or end of an age)
* reported speech
* repeated actions
* continued actions
* interrupted actions (the interrupting action is normally expressed with the preterit)

Examples:
Quando eu tinha cinco anos morava em São Paulo.
When I was five years old, I lived in São Paulo.

Quando o menino estava doente, não queria tomar os seus medicamentos de três em três horas.
When the child was sick, he didn't want to take his medicine every three hours.

Eram cinco da tarde.
It was five o'clock.

Note: the imperfect is also used to show politeness in spoken discourse, where it replaces the conditional:

Por favor, podia abrir a janela?
Please, could you open the window?

Some verbs have different meanings when used in the imperfect as opposed to the preterite.

* **querer** (to want)

Examples:
Nós queríamos convidar esse casal.
We wanted to invite that couple. (We *intended* to invite that couple.)

Nós quisemos convidar esse casal.
We wanted to invite that couple. (We *tried* but encountered some obstacle, e.g. didn't have their phone number.)

- *conhecer* (to know/to meet)

Examples:
Gilberto já conhecia o treinador.
Gilberto already knew the coach.

Gilberto conheceu o treinador ontem.
Gilberto met the coach yesterday.

The verb *saber* in Portuguese works in a similar way: *sabia* means "to know" and *soube* means "to find out."

- *ter* + *que* (to have to)

Examples:
Julião e Martinho tinham que encontrar uma solução.
Julião e Martinho had to find a solution.

Julião e Martinho tiveram que encontrar uma solução.
Julião e Martinho had to find a solution (and they found one).

The verb *poder* in Portuguese works in a similar way: [eu] *pude* conveys greater resolve and sense of completion than *podia*.

5.1.4 Future tense

The simple future tense (*Futuro* or *Futuro do Presente*) is not as commonly used in spoken discourse as the periphrastic form *ir* + infinitive. However, it is still the standard form in written formal discourse. The future is used to express an action in the future, as in English, and also to express conjecture in the present or future. The form is made by adding the following endings to the infinitive:

	-ar	*-er*	*-ir*
eu		-ei	
tu		-ás	
você, ele, ela		- á	
nós		-emos	
vocês, eles, elas		-ão	

The following verbs have an irregular root for the formation of both the future and the conditional:

dizer (to say), **eu direi**, etc.
fazer (to do or make), **eu farei**, etc.
trazer (to bring), **eu trarei**, etc.

Examples:
Augusto será com certeza um bom médico.
Augusto certainly will be a good doctor.

Um dia regressarei à minha cidade natal.
Some day I'll return to my native town.

Segundo a Bíblia, o mundo acabará pelo fogo.
According to the Bible, the world will end by fire.

Será que ele disse mesmo isso?
Did he really say that? (I wonder if he really said that.)

5.1.5 The conditional

The conditional (*Condicional* or *Futuro do Pretérito*) is used both in hypothetical situations (contrary to fact) in the present, to express politeness, and to express the future in the past.

	-ar	*-er*	*-ir*
eu		-ia	
tu		-ias	
você, ele, ela		-ia	
nós		-íamos	
vocês, eles, elas		-iam	

Examples:
Eu gostaria muito de visitar Salvador e Recife.
I would love to visit Salvador and Recife.

Poderia fazer-me um favor?
Could you do me a favor?

Se eu fosse rico, então compraria uma casa grande.
If I were rich, then I would buy a big house.

Ela disse-me ontem que viria visitar-me hoje.
She told me yesterday that she would visit me today.

Note: in informal contexts, the imperfect indicative is used instead.

5.1.6 The personal infinitive

The personal infinitive (*infinitivo pessoal* or *flexionado*) is formed by adding the endings below to the final *–r* of the infinitive. The endings are the same for all three groups of verbs.

	-ar	-er	-ir
eu		–	
tu		-es	
você, ele, ela		–	
nós		-mos	
vocês, eles, elas		-em	

The personal infinitive is used in subordinate clauses only after certain conjunctions, and only when the subject of the subordinate clause is different from that of the main clause; otherwise the ordinary infinitive is used. The uses of the personal infinitive are often similar to the uses of the present and imperfect subjunctive, except that there is no *que* at the beginning of the subordinate clause.

1. With *para* (in order to)

    Example:

    Para nós podermos pedir um empréstimo, o proprietário da casa tem de dar um preço para nós o mais depressa possível.

    For us to be able to apply for a mortgage loan, the house owner has to give us a quote as soon as possible.

2. With *por* (because)

    Example:

    Por elas serem meio esquecidas é que Daniel ligou a lembrar da reunião.

    Because [of the fact that] they are forgetful, Daniel called to remind [them] of the meeting.

3. With *ao*

    Example:

    Ao mudarem a mesa de lugar, uma das pernas caiu.

    As they were moving the table, one of its legs fell off.

4. With *sem* (without)

    Example:

    Sem saberem quando você se vai embora, eles não podem fazer planos para a ida ao Porto.

    Without knowing when you're leaving, they can't plan their trip to Oporto.

5. With *antes de* (before, until)

    Example:

    Antes de os alunos saberem nadar, o instrutor não os deixa ir para a piscina grande.

    Until the students learn to swim, the instructor will not let them in the big swimming pool.

6. With *depois de* (after)

    Examples:

    A luz faltou 10 minutos depois de eles chegarem.

    There was a power outage (power cut) ten minutes after they arrived home.

**Depois de os pais fecharem a porta é que as crianças se
lembraram que queriam ir no banheiro.** (Br)
After the parents had locked the door, the children remembered that
they wanted to go to the bathroom.

7. With impersonal constructions such as *é possível* (it is possible), *é triste*
    (it's sad), etc.

    Examples:
    É conveniente telefonares a saber a se o voo não foi cancelado.
    (Pt)
    It's convenient that you [should] call to find out whether the flight was
    canceled.

    É boa ideia eles chegarem meia-hora antes.
    It's a good idea for them to arrive half an hour earlier.

8. With a nominalized verb (variation of the previous case)
    Example:
    Aprenderem chinês pode ser útil no futuro.
    It may be useful in the future for [you/them] to learn Chinese.

9. With an anaphoric structure using the preposition *a*, or emphasizing
    the subject.
    Example:
    **"O 8 de Março é o nosso dia [da Mulher]. Somos nós a
    definirmos a maneira como queremos comemorá-lo"** (M. I.
    Casa, *NoTMoC: Notícias de Moçambique*, 7 April 1999).
    March 8 is our day [Women's Day]. We are the ones to define the
    manner in which we want to commemorate it.

10. With the preposition *de* in various structures, as long as it involves a
    different subject in each clause, or a different emphasis.
    Example:
    **"A proposta veio de constatarmos que, na tradição makhuwa,
    são principalmente as mulheres a fazerem as cerimónias de
    Makeya e que elas representam o vínculo com os
    antepassados"** (M. I. Casa, *NoTMoC: Notícias de Moçambique*,
    7 April 1999).
    The proposition arose from our realizing that, in the Makhuwa
    tradition, it's mostly the women who do the Makeya ceremonies and
    they represent the link with the ancestors.

    Note that in the second phrase of this example, the personal infinitive is
    linked to the periphrastic progressive construction (see Section 5.8.2)
    typical of European and Lusophone African Portuguese.

    Note: As is evident in the examples just given, the personal infinitive,
    unlike the subjunctive, does not require tense agreement between
    subordinate and subordinating clauses.

5.2   Compound indicative mode tenses

The perfect tenses (*tempos compostos*) in Portuguese are formed with the verb *ter* combined with the past participle of the verb being used. For the formation and use of the two types of past participle in Portuguese, see Section 5.5.2.

5.2.1   Present perfect

The present perfect (*Pretérito Perfeito Composto*) is used to express an action that began in the recent past and has not yet been completed. However, it cannot be used simply to substitute for the simple preterite as in French, Italian, and Spanish spoken in Spain. Its use is much more similar to that of Latin American Spanish and to English present perfect. The present tense of *ter* is used. The verb *ter*, in the present, functions as an auxiliary.

Examples:
Ultimamente tenho feito muito exercício.
I have exercised a lot lately.

Eles não têm visto o Rogério. A última vez que o viram foi há um ano.
They haven't seen Rogério (recently). The last time they saw him was a year ago.

5.2.2   Pluperfect

The pluperfect (*Pretérito Mais-que-Perfeito*) has two forms, one simple and one compound (*composto*). The pluperfect tense is usually used with another verb in the past (never just by itself, unless the rest of the sentence is implied) to express an action that occurred before another action in the past. The compound form is the more commonly used of the two. It is made by combining the imperfect tense of *ter* with the past participle of the main verb.

Examples:
Maria já tinha nascido quando o homem–chegou à lua.
Maria had already been born when man arrived on the moon.

O ladrão já tinha fugido quando a polícia chegou.
The thief had already escaped when the police arrived.

The pluperfect can also be used in a negative sentence to indicate an action which had not yet happened when another action took place.

145

Example:
Manuel ainda não tinha saído quando eu lhe telefonei.
Manuel had not yet left when I called him.

The simple pluperfect is primarily used in written discourse. It has its own conjugation, formed by adding the endings below to the infinitive:

	-ar	*-er*	*-ir*
eu	-a		
tu	-as		
você, ele, ela	-a		
nós	-amos		
vocês, eles, elas	-aram		

Note: the only difference in pronunciation between the forms *falaras/falara* and the future forms *falarás/falará* is the stress:

ele falara (he had spoken); *ele falará* (he will speak)
tu falaras (you had spoken); *tu falarás* (you will speak).

5.2.3 Future Perfect

The future perfect (*Futuro do Presente Composto*) is used to express a future action which is completed before another action in the future. The future tense of *ter* is used, with the past participle of the main verb. It can also be used to express doubt about the past.

Examples:
Aos 50 anos, já terei viajado muito.
I will have traveled a lot by the time I'm 50.

O Afonso chega às 8 de avião. O meu voo sai às 6, portanto quando o Afonso chegar, eu já terei partido.
Afonso will arrive at 8 by plane. My flight leaves at 6, so by the time Afonso arrives I will have left.

Será que eles já terão ido a esse restaurante?
I wonder if they have gone to that restaurant.

5.2.4 Conditional perfect

The conditional perfect (*Condicional Composto* or *Futuro do Pretérito Composto*) is usually used to express the hypothetical result of a conditional (unreal) situation in the past. The conditional form of *ter* is used.

Examples:
Eu teria ido à praia se não tivesse chovido.
I would have gone to the beach if it hadn't rained.

Se eles não tivessem estudado tanto para o exame, não teriam tido uma boa nota.

If they had not studied so much for the exam, they would not have received a high grade.

The conditional perfect is also used to express conjecture in the past.

Example:

Como teriam descoberto?

I wonder how they found out.

5.3 The simple subjunctive mode tenses

The subjunctive mode (*conjuntivo* or *subjuntivo*) is primarily used in subordinate clauses, when there is a change of subject, after expressions and verbs which denote doubt, emotion, negation, or influence. The two clauses are usually connected by the conjunction *que*. It is also used in adjectival clauses with unspecific antecedents, and after some adverbial conjunctions. There are three simple subjunctive tenses in Portuguese: imperfect, present, and future.

Some examples of these expressions include:

1. Doubt: *duvidar* (to doubt), *não achar* (to not believe), *é duvidoso* (it is doubtful that), *talvez* (maybe – this does not take *que*)

   Examples:

   Duvido que ele chegue a tempo.

   I doubt that he will arrive on time.

   Talvez ela esteja sob a influência de espíritos malignos.

   Maybe she is under the the influence of evil spirits.

2. Negation or refusal: *negar* (to deny), *não é* (it is not), *não dizer [que]* (to not say [that]), *não é verdade* (it is not true), *recusar* (to refuse), *não aceitar* (to not accept)

   Example:

   A pobre mulher negou que o seu marido fosse o culpado.

   The poor woman denied that her husband was guilty.

3. Emotion: *alegrar-se* (to be happy), *estar triste* (to be sad), *lamentar* (to be sorry), *estar furioso* (to be angry)

   Example:

   Lamento que não estejas comigo. (Pt)

   I am sorry that you are not with me.

4. Influence: *mandar* (to command), *exigir* (to order), *dizer* (to tell – only when an indirect command is expressed), *pedir* (to request), *fazer*

com (to make [someone do something]), *impedir* (to prevent something), *querer* (to want [something to happen])

Examples:
Quero que você me faça um favor.
I want you to do me a favor.

A mãe sempre dizia às filhas que não saíssem sozinhas.
The mother always told her daughters not to go out alone.

Ele impediu que eu fizesse um grande erro.
He prevented me from committing a great error.

Note: When *querer* combines with a verb of information (*saber*, to know, *conhecer*, to know), it no longer takes the subjunctive.

Example:
Quero saber o que eles fizeram para terem tanto sucesso.
I want to know what they did to have so much success.

5. Unspecific or unknown antecedents: the subjunctive is used if the object referred to in the clause is either unspecific or cannot actually be named because it is unknown.

Examples:
Pedro quer conhecer uma mulher que fale sete línguas.
Peter wants to meet a woman who speaks seven languages.

Quero uma casa que tenha quatro quartos e uma sala grande.
I want a house that has four bedrooms and a large living room.

Note: If the antecedent is specific or known, the indicative is used:

Procuro o meu livro que tem a capa vermelha.
I am looking for my book that has the red cover.

6. After *antes de* (before) and *depois que* (after).

Example:
Dá-me o dinheiro que tens antes que eu te dê um tiro. (Pt)
Give me the money you have before I shoot you.

7. To express finality with *para que* (so that), *a fim de que* (so that).

8. To express concession with *embora* (although), *ainda que* (even if), *mesmo que* (even if).

Example:
Mesmo que me dês mil escudos, não te empresto o meu carro.
Even if you give me ten thousand escudos, I won't lend you my car.

Note: For actions or events that concern a moment in the future and are conveyed using similar constructions to the above, please refer to Section 5.3.3 (Future subjunctive).

5.3.1 Present subjunctive

The present subjunctive (*Presente do Conjuntivo Subjuntivo*) is used after a main verb in the present to express an action or state in the present or future.

The root of present subjunctive forms is the first person singular (*eu*) form of the present indicative. Verbs with irregular forms in the present therefore retain this irregularity in the present subjunctive. The endings are the following:

	-ar	*-er* and *-ir*
eu	-e	-a
tu	-es	-as
você, ele, ela	-e	-a
nós	-emos	-amos
vocês, eles, elas	-em	-am

The following verbs have irregular roots in the present subjunctive:

querer (to want): **eu queira**, etc.
saber (to know): **eu saiba**, etc.
ser (to be): **eu seja**, etc.
estar (to be): **eu esteja**, etc.
ir (to go): **eu vá**, etc.
haver (impersonal – "there is," "there exists"): **haja**.

Examples:
Talvez eu também possa ir.
Maybe I can go too.

É pena que ele não fale inglês.
It's a shame that he does not speak English.

Recomendo que você vá no Brasil no Ano Novo.
I recommend that you go to Brazil for the New Year.

5.3.2 Past subjunctive

The past subjunctive (*Pretérito Imperfeito do Conjuntivo/Subjuntivo*) is formed from the third person plural of the preterite whose last syllable is replaced by the endings below. The endings are the same for the three groups of verbs.

	-ar	*-er*	*-ir*
eu		-sse	
tu		-sses	
você, ele, ela		-sse	
nós		-ssemos	
vocês, eles, elas		-ssem	

Example: **dizer** (to say/to tell): **eu dissesse**.

The past subjunctive is used after verbs and expressions which require the subjunctive in the past, and also in the conditional in hypothetical statements concerning the present which are contrary to fact.

Examples:
Embora não se queixasse, ela tinha frequentemente dores de estômago.
Even though she did not complain, she often suffered from stomach pains.

Se eu tivesse muito dinheiro, compraria uma casa nova.
If I had a lot of money, I would buy a new house.

Me falaram que fosse à entrevista às 2 horas. (Br)
They told me to go to the interview at 2 p.m.

5.3.3 Future subjunctive

The root of the forms for the future subjunctive (*Futuro do Conjuntivo/Subjuntivo*) is that of the third person plural of the preterit. The *–am* of the form is replaced by the endings given in the table. They are the same for all three groups of verbs.

	-ar	*-er*	*-ir*
eu		–	
tu		-es	
você, ele, ela		–	
nós		-mos	
vocês, eles, elas		-em	

The future subjunctive is used to express the future in the subordinate clause only after certain conjunctions, namely *se*, *enquanto*, *quando*, and the expressions *sempre que* and *o que*.

Examples:
Tudo o que quiserem dar será bem-vindo.
Anything that they want to give will be well received.

Me liga amanhã quando tu acordar (Br, reg)
Call me tomorrow when you wake up.

Enquanto não nos reembolsarem, não podemos ir de férias.
Until they pay us back, we can't go on vacation.

5.4   Compound subjunctive mode tenses

Compound tenses are made up of two verbal forms: the past participle of the main verb, combined with the appropriately conjugated form of the auxiliary verb *ter* (*tenha feito*, *tivesse feito*, *tiver feito*).

The use of a compound tense usually means that there are two actions involved and that one takes place prior to the other.

The compound tenses in the subjunctive are principally used in the same cases as their indicative counterparts but after the expressions which always elicit the subjunctive in the simple tense.

5.4.1   Present perfect subjunctive

The Present Subjunctive of *ter* is used, combined with the past participle of the verb you want to use.

The present perfect subjunctive (*Pretérito Perfeito do Conjuntivo / Subjuntivo Composto*) is used to express an action anterior to an action in the present after any of the verbs or expressions that elicit the subjunctive mode. It is only used in subordinate clauses or after *talvez*.

Examples:

Não acho que os meus alunos tenham estudado o suficiente para o exame.

I don't think that my students have studied enough for the exam.

Vamos almoçar no Mario's, espero que Tânia tenha reservado uma mesa ontem.

Let's have lunch at Mario's, I hope Tânia reserved a table.

5.4.2   Pluperfect subjunctive

The imperfect subjunctive of *ter* is used combined with the past participle of the verb you want to use.

The pluperfect or past perfect subjunctive (*o Pretérito Mais-que-Perfeito do Conjuntivo / Subjuntivo*) is used to express an action which occurred before another action in the past after verbs which take the subjunctive, and also in hypothetical situations contrary to fact in the past.

With hypothetical situations, the pluperfect subjunctive may combine with the conditional perfect or the conditional depending on whether the result is in the past or present.

Examples:

Se eu tivesse nascido na Alemanha, teria aprendido alemão desde criança.

If I had been born in Germany, I would have learned German as a child.

151

Se eu tivesse nascido na Alemanha, hoje falaria alemão fluentemente.
If I had been born in Germany, today I would be able to speak German fluently.

This tense is often used with reported speech in the past.

Example:
O inspe(c)tor disse que não acreditava que o suspeito tivesse saído do prédio antes de o assassinato se dar.
The inspector stated that he did not believe that the suspect had left the building before the murder was committed.

5.4.3 Future perfect subjunctive

The future perfect subjunctive (*Futuro Composto do Conjuntivo / Subjuntivo*) is used to express an action which is completed before another action in the future, after the same expressions that take the simple future subjunctive. The future subjunctive of *ter* is used.

Examples:
Assim que o avião tiver atingido uma altitude estável, se servirão as bebidas.
As soon as the plane has reached cruising altitude, the drinks will be served.

Quando tiveres acabado o exame, podes fazer as perguntas que quiseres. (Pt)
When you have finished the exam, then you can ask all the questions you like.

5.5 Present and past participles

5.5.1 The present participle

The present participle is formed by adding *–ante* to all *–ar* verbs, and *–ente* to all *–er* and *–ir* verbs.
 While it is not used as frequently as in English, several present participles are used as substantives in everyday speech.
Examples:

---

a nascente (the water spring)
a parturiente (the woman in labor)
a vidente (the clairvoyant)
o nascente (the sunrise)
o poente (the sunset)
o poluente (the polluting agent)

o/a **amante** (the lover)
o/a **assaltante** (the robber)
o/a **assinante** (the subscriber)
o/a **assistente** (the assistant)
o/a **transeunte** (the walker, passer-by) (Pt)

5.5.2 The past participle

The past participle is formed by adding the ending –*ado* to the root of
–*ar* verbs, and –*ido* to the root of –*er* and –*ir* verbs.
 The following verbs have irregular past participles:

abrir (aberto)
cobrir (coberto)
dizer (dito)
escrever (escrito)
fazer (feito)
pôr (posto)
ver (visto)
vir (vindo)

Some verbs in Portuguese have two participles, one irregular and one
regular. The irregular forms, in these cases, are used as adjectives with
the verb *estar*, while the regular forms combine with the verb *ter* in the
perfect tenses, or the verb *ser* in the passive voice.

	Regular form	Irregular form
aceitar	aceitado	aceite (Pt); aceito/a (Br)
acender	acendido	aceso
eleger	elegido	eleito
emergir	emergido	emerso
entregar	entregado	entregue
expressar	expressado	expresso
extinguir	extinguido	extinto
ganhar	ganhado	ganho
gastar	gastado	gasto
imprimir	imprimido	impresso
inserir	inserido	inserto
morrer	morrido	morto
omitir	omitido	omisso
pagar	pagado	pago
romper	rompido	roto
salvar	salvado	salvo

Note: When functioning as adjectives, the participles must agree with the nouns they modify.

Examples:
A loteria foi ganha por um grupo de sete pessoas.
The lottery was won by a group of seven people.

Note: In many cases the irregular past participle can be used as a noun.

Example:
O morto foi levado para a morgue.
The dead man was taken to the morgue.

5.6 Imperative

The imperative is used to give commands. There are forms for the second person singular and plural (both informal and formal); the first person plural (we) takes the corresponding subjunctive form of the present. The subject pronoun is omitted.

Note: in European Portuguese, the unstressed (clitic) pronouns follow affirmative commands and precede negative commands.

Examples:
Passa-me o sal.
Pass me the salt.

Não te atrases.
Don't be late.

Não me digas mentiras.
Don't tell me lies.

5.6.1 Second person informal (*tu*)

The affirmative command for the second person informal of regular verbs is the *tu* form of the present indicative, with the *–s* removed.

Examples:
Come! (Eat!)
Fala! (Speak!)

The following verbs have irregular imperative forms:

ser (to be): **sê.**
dizer (to say): **diz.**
fazer (to do/to make): **faz.**

The negative commands share the form of the present subjunctive.

Example:
Não comas tão depressa!
Don't eat so fast!

5.6.2 Other imperative forms

All other imperative forms are the same as the present subjunctive without the subject pronoun.

Examples:
Vamos! (Let's go!)

A mãe disse-lhes "Não falem com desconhecidos!"
The mother told them, "Don't talk to strangers!"

5.7 The gerund

The gerund (*Gerúndio*) is formed by removing the final *–r* from the infinitive and adding *–ndo*.
    The gerund may be used after the verb *estar* to form the present progressive (in Brazilian Portuguese) and it is also used to substitute the structure *Quando*/When + conjugated verb for synthesis when the following clause shares the same subject.

Examples:
Estou comendo. (Br)
I am eating.

Ele comia, pondo rapidamente a comida na boca.
He ate, rapidly shoving the food into his mouth.

5.8 Periphrastic verb forms

There are three periphrastic structures (formed by a verb and an infinitive).

5.8.1 Continuous tenses

The continuous tenses in Portugal are formed with *estar + a +* infinitive in the present, past, or future. In Brazil, they are formed with *estar +* gerund. They are used to show an action in progress while it is occurring.

Examples:

Estou falando no telefone. Pode baixar esse som? (Br)
I'm speaking on the phone. Can you turn that noise down?

Mariana estava a ler o jornal quando alguém bateu à porta. (Pt)
Mariana was reading the newspaper when someone knocked on the door.

5.8.2 The progressive tenses

The progressive tenses are formed by *ir* + infinitive and are the equivalents of the English "to be going" + infinitive. These are the equivalents of the future simple and the future in the past. This form tends to replace the simple future in spoken discourse.

Example:
Eu ia sair quando o telefone tocou.
I was going to leave when the phone rang.

5.8.3 Acabar de

Acabar de means "(to have) just" and expresses the idea that an action has recently been completed.

Example:
Acabo de chegar.
I (have) just arrived.

5.9 *Ser*, *estar*, and *ficar*

Ser, estar, and *ficar* are all equivalents of "to be" but each expresses different aspects.

5.9.1 Location

Estar is used to express temporary locations. *Ficar* may also be used to express the idea of "to stay."

Example:
Estou em casa neste momento.
I am at home at this moment.

Ser is used to express a permanent location, and is therefore used only in the case of geographic locations, buildings, etc. It is not used to express the location of moveable objects, animals, or people.

Example:
O Brasil é na América do Sul.
Brazil is in South America.

Ficar is also used to express permanent locations and can also mean "to stay."

Examples:
Angola fica na África.
Angola is in Africa.

Eu fiquei em casa quando a minha família foi de férias.
I stayed home when my family went on vacation.

5.9.2 Description

Estar is used to express variable conditions, both physical and mental.

Examples:
Estou cansado
I am tired (now).

O doente que sofre de cancro está muito magro.
The cancer patient is very thin.

Ser is used to express permanent characteristics.

Examples:
A Luciana é uma pessoa feliz.
Luciana is a happy person (it is part of her personality).

O meu pai é muito magro. Come muito, mas nunca engorda.
My father is a very thin man. He eats a lot but never gains weight.

Ficar is used to express a change in condition or to mean "to become."

Examples:
O céu ficou muito escuro de repente com a aproximação da trovoada.
The sky suddenly became dark with the approaching storm.

O Patrício ficou muito contente com a notícia.
Patrick was very happy with the news.

5.9.3 Special uses of *ser*

Ser has several special uses in Portuguese, many of which require the preposition *de*.

1. Possession
   Este disco é do Marcos.
   This cd is Mark's.

2. Origin
   Ela é de Bissau.
   She is from Bissau.

3. Composition
   Só gosto de camisas de algodão.
   I only like cotton shirts.

   Esta cadeira é de plástico e metal.
   This chair is made of metal and plastic.

4. Time
   Ser is used to show clock time, seasons and times of the year, days,
   dates, holidays, etc.
   Era Natal quando te conheci.
   It was Christmas when I met you.

   Será Verão quando acabar de ler *Os Maias*.
   It will be summer when I finish *The Maias* (a famous, but lengthy,
   Portuguese novel by Eça de Queirós).

   É uma da tarde.
   It is one o'clock.

5. Nationality
   Paulo é Moçambicano.
   Paul is Mozambican.

6. Religion
   Sou católica.
   I am catholic.

7. Political affiliation
   Ela costumava ser comunista.
   She used to be a communist.

8. Impersonal expressions
   When combining with impersonal expressions, *ser* is always conjugated
   in the third person singular.
   É fabuloso que o governo apoie a cultura.
   It is wonderful that the government supports culture.

5.9.4 Special uses of *estar*

The following expressions are made with *estar* + *com* followed by a
noun. They may also be expressed by the verb *ter* which at times
indicates a more lasting condition.

estar com fome (to be hungry)
estar com sede (to be thirsty)
estar com frio (to be cold)
estar com calor (to be hot)
estar com saudades (to miss somebody or something)
estar com dores (to have a pain)

5.10 *Saber* and *conhecer*

Saber and *conhecer* are both equivalents of the English "to know."
Conhecer generally expresses familiarity with an object, concept, or
person, while *saber* expresses memorized knowledge or combines with
the infinitive to mean "to know how to do something."

Examples with *conhecer*:
Conheço as obras de Jorge Amado.
I know (am familiar with) the works of Jorge Amado (a well-known
Brazilian author).

O meu primo conhece a Marta.
My cousin knows Marta.

Note: With geographic locations, *conhecer* also expresses the fact that
someone has visited the place.

Example:
Conhecem Brasília?
Do you know Brasilia?

Examples with *saber*:
Quando era criança, tinha que saber a tabuada de cor.
When I was child, I had to know my multiplication tables by heart.

Ele é a(c)tor e por isso sabe de certo *Hamlet*.
He is an actor, so he certainly knows *Hamlet* (has it memorized).

Sei nadar.
I know how to swim; I can swim.

Note: there are two special constructions with *saber*:

Saber de means to "know of" or "to find out about" something; *saber
que* means "to know that."

Examples:
Souberam do terremoto na China?
Did you hear about the earthquake in China?

Sei que me estás a mentir. (Pt)
I know that you're lying to me.

5.11   Modal verbs

Modal verbs are those which combine with another verb in the infinitive form in order to express intentions or opinions. In English, some examples are "can," "should," "might," and "must." The chief difference between English and Portuguese auxiliaries is that in Portuguese, the auxiliaries can normally be conjugated in all tenses, while in English they cannot.

The following are modal verbs in Portuguese: *há que, dever, ter que/de*, and *poder*.

Há que is an impersonal expression which corresponds to the idea of "one must." It expresses obligation or urgency with consequences if not obeyed. The agent making the demand is not expressed or necessary and may be supposed to be "The powers that be."

Example:
Há que entregar as requisições a tempo se queremos ter os livros no início do ano.
We must (it is absolutely necessary to) turn in the requests on time if we want the books by the beginning of the year.

Dever is a conjugated verb which corresponds to "should." It expresses an opinion with an inherent suggestion. It does not, however, express a command.

Examples:
Você deve ir ao médico.
You should go to the doctor (but you are not forced or obliged to).

In the imperfect, *dever* conveys a weaker sense than in the present indicative, unless the imperfect is part of a reported speech structure.

Example:
Meu irmão disse que eu devia investir mais dinheiro na minha conta de reforma. (Pt)
My brother told me that I should invest more money in my retirement plan.

Ter que (also *ter de*) corresponds to "have to" and indicates obligation but is more personal.

Examples:
Tenho que me ir embora às cinco horas sem falta.
I have to leave at 5 without fail.

A minha mãe disse-me que eu tinha de limpar o meu quarto este fim de semana.
My mother told me that I had to clean my room this weekend.

Poder corresponds to "can" or "could" and indicates a possible act on the part of the agent.

Example:
Você pode ir comigo às compras amanhã?
Can (could) you come shopping with me tomorrow?

Pode ser que / podia ser que is an impersonal expression that corresponds to "might" and indicate a possibility but with less certainty than *poder* by itself.

Example:
Pode ser que o avião chegue atrasado por causa da tempestade.
The plane might arrive late, due to the storm.

5.12   Passive voice

Portuguese has two ways of expressing the passive voice, one which is similar to the English use of "to be + participle + agent + by" and the other which employs the passive *se*.

Ser + participle + *por* + agent

The passive voice with *ser* is not as commonly used as its English counterpart. It is normally used only in simple tenses (present, preterit and, less commonly, future) and is generally used when the agent is explicitly mentioned. In this case the participle must agree with the subject of the sentence (which is the receiver or result of the action done).

Examples:
O poema *Os Lusíadas* foi escrito por Camões.
The poem *The Lusiads* was written by Camoens.

Duas cidades foram destruídas por um vulcão.
Two cities were destroyed by a volcano.

Os participantes serão apresentados pelo Presidente.
The participants will be presented by the President.

Passive *se*

The passive with *se* (*pronome apassivante*) is the more commonly used of the two passive forms. It can be used with any tense but, when used, the agent (or doer) must be implied and not given explicitly in the sentence: if it is, the active voice must be used. The verb is conjugated in the third person singular or plural to agree with the receiver of the action. This construction can also be used as the equivalent of the indefinite impersonal subjects "you," "one," or "they" in English.

Examples:

Durante a guerra destruiu-se muita propriedade.
During the war, a great deal of property was destroyed.

Vende-se livros baratos naquela livraria (or Vendem-se livros . . .).
They sell inexpensive books in that store.

Fala-se português em cinco países da África.
Portuguese is spoken in five countries in Africa.

Desculpe, não se pode fumar no autocarro. (Pt)
Excuse me, you cannot smoke on the bus.

6 Reported speech

6.1 Direct reported speech

Direct reported speech receives the same punctuation as in English and is separated from the rest of the sentence by a comma and quotation marks. In Portuguese, other punctuation marks are not left inside the quotation marks.

Maria disse, "Estou muito zangada contigo".
Maria said, "I am very angry at you."

6.2 Indirect reported speech

In cases where quoted discourse is incorporated into the sentence, any agreements between the quoted material and other introductory text must be respected.

Indirect discourse is usually introduced by the following expressions:

Statements:	**dizer que** (to say that)
	declarar que (to declare that)
	explicar que (to explain that)
	esclarecer que (to clarify that)
	insinuar que (to insinuate that)
	responder que (to answer that)
	exclamar que (to exclaim that)
	negar que (to deny that)
Questions:	**perguntar se** (to ask if)
	tentar saber se/quando/como/por que (to try to find out + any interrogative word)

If the reporting verb is in the present, then all verb tenses remain the same. If the reporting verb is in the past, then all reported speech must shift tense accordingly.

Present Tense	**Imperfect**
"Vou ao cinema."	Ele disse que ia ao cinema.
I am going to the movies.	He said that he was going to the movies.
Imperfect	**Imperfect**
"Ia ao cinema."	Ele disse que ia ao cinema.
I was going to the movies.	He said that he was going to the movies.
Preterit	**Pluperfect**
"Fui . . ."	Ele disse que tinha ido ao cinema.
I went . . .	He said that he had gone to the movies.
Future	**Conditional**
"Irei . . ."	Ele disse que iria . . .
I will go . . .	He said that he would go . . .
Future Subjunctive	**Imperfect subjunctive**
"Quando eu for . . ."	Ele disse que quando fosse . . .
When I go . . .	He said that when he would go . . .
Present subjunctive	**Imperfect subjunctive**
"Talvez vá . . ."	Ele disse que talvez fosse . . .
Maybe I will go . . .	He said that he might go . . .
Imperative	**Imperfect subjunctive**
"Volta depressa, Helena!"	Ele disse a Helena que voltasse depressa.
Come back soon, Helen!	Note: The following form may also be used: *para* + personal inf.
	Ele disse a Elena para voltar depressa.

The following adverbial expressions of time and location must also be modified in reported speech:

"Fico **aqui**."	Disse que ficava **ali/naquele lugar**.
"I am staying **here**."	He said that he was staying **there/in that place**.
"Fico **ali**."	Disse que ficava **ali**.
"I am staying **there**."	He said that he was staying **there**.

"Vou **agora**."	Disse que ia **naquele momento**.
"I am going **now**."	He said that he was going **at that moment**.
"Vou **hoje**."	Disse que ia **naquele dia**.
"I am going **today**."	He said that was going **that day**.
"Vou **amanhã**."	Disse que ia **no dia seguinte**.
"I am going **tomorrow**."	He said that he was going **the next day**.
"Vou **depois de amanhã**."	Disse que ia **daí a dois dias**.
"I am going **the day after tomorrow**."	He said that he was going **two days later**.
"Vou **no próximo mês**."	Disse que ia **no mês seguinte**.
I am going **next month**.	
	He said that he was going **the next month**.

7 Pronouns and articles

7.1 Articles

Articles in Portuguese agree with the nouns they modify in the same manner as adjectives.

7.1.1 Indefinite article

The indefinite article corresponds to the English "a, an." The plural forms express the idea of "some" and are often omitted when their meaning can easily be implied. The forms are the following:

uma – f sg	**um** – m sg
umas – f pl	**uns** – m pl

Examples:
Tenho uma irmã.
I have a sister.

Comprei uns sapatos novos.
I bought some new shoes.

Note: The indefinite article may be omitted before the word *outro* (other), unlike in English when it combines as "another."

Comprei uma camisa de que gosto muito e por isso comprei outra hoje.
I bought a shirt that I liked a lot so today I bought **another**.

7.1.2 Definite article

The definite article corresponds to the English "the." Its forms are the following:

a – f sg	**o** – m sg
as – f pl	**os** – m pl

The definite article creates a contraction with the following words:

de (of, from)	**do, da, dos, das**
a (to, at)	**ao, à, aos, às**
em (in, on)	**no, na, nos, nas**
por (for, by)	**pelo, pela, pelos, pelas**
aquele (that – adjective)	**àquele, àquela, àqueles, àquelas**
aquilo (that – pronoun)	**àquilo**

The definite article has several uses which are specialized in Portuguese:

1. It is used to emphasize a noun that is part of a phrase showing possession.

    Example:
    Este é o livro do estudante.
    This is the student's book [as opposed to another book].

2. In Portugal and Africa, the definite article is used before possessive adjectives. It is used before the possessive pronoun in all variants of Portuguese.

    Examples:
    O meu nome é Josué.
    My name is Joshua.

    Tenho as minhas chaves. Tens as tuas?
    I have my keys. Do you have yours?

3. In Portugal and Africa, but not always in Brazil, the definite article is used before people's names when they are not being addressed directly.

    Examples:
    O Carlos chegou atrasado.
    Carlos arrived late.

    A Penélope é muito inteligente.
    Penelope is very intelligent.

    Note: The article is not used before the name of famous writers as a sign of respect.

4. The definite article is used before the following geographical names:

• Countries, except for Portugal, Cuba, Israel, and the African Luso-phone countries, with the exception of Guinea-Bissau.

Fui ao Japão e depois visitei Moçambique.
I went to Japan and then I visited Mozambique.

• Oceans, rivers, lakes, mountains, continents and islands, and the points of the compass (north, south, east, west).

O rio Mississippi fica na América do Norte.
The Mississippi River is in North America.

• Parks.

Fomos ao Parque Chico Mendes quando estivemos no Brasil.
We went to Chico Mendes park when we were in Brazil.

5. The definite article is used when a group in its totality, or a general concept, are presented at the beginning of a sentence. The article is omitted if the noun is not at the beginning.

Examples:
O amor é belo.
Love is beautiful.

Os cães ladram muito. (Pt)
Dogs bark a lot.

A penicilina é um medicamento importante.
Penicillin is an important medicine.

Não gosto de carne de vaca.
I don't like beef.

6. The definite article is used before the names of diseases.

Example:
A tuberculose matou muita gente durante o século XIX.
Tuberculosis killed many people during the nineteenth century.

7.2 Pronouns

In Portuguese, as in English, pronouns are used to substitute for a noun or noun phrase. Here they will be discussed according to their syntactic function within the sentence.

7.2.1 Subject pronouns

Subject pronouns in Portuguese are stressed. They generally precede a verb and may stand alone in spoken discourse. They may be omitted before any verb unless they are needed to clarify the subject of the verb.

The subject pronouns are the following:

1st person sg	**eu** – I
2nd person sg	Equivalents of "you"
	Informal:
	tu (mostly used in Portugal and Lusophone Africa), but also in a few areas of Brazil, although not always followed by the corresponding verb forms: *tu vai* "you go."
	você (is used in informal address in Brazil)
	Formal:
	você (in Portugal and Lusophone Africa)
3rd person sg	**ele** – he; **ela** – she
	Note: The subject pronoun "it" is not used in Portuguese. Instead the subject may be omitted or replaced by *ele* or *ela*.
1st person pl	**nós** – we
2nd person pl	**vocês** – you
3rd person pl	**eles** – they (masculine); **elas** (feminine)

For more on the differences in the use of *você* in Portugal and Brazil, see Section 3.5.

7.2.2 Object pronouns

There are two basic groups of object pronouns, those that combine with verbs, and those which follow prepositions.

• Pronouns combining with prepositions are stressed and only combine with other words in the cases marked below.

1st person sg – me	**mim**
2nd person sg – you	**ti**
	você
3rd person sg – him, her	**ele**
	ela
1st person pl – us	**nós**
2nd person pl – you	**vocês**
3rd person pl – them	**eles**
	elas

These pronouns follow their prepositions.

Example:
Isto é para ti.
This is for you.

Note: Pronouns following the preposition *com* (with) form:

Com +	
mim	**comigo**
ti	**contigo**
você	**consigo** (Pt, formal register)
ele	**com ele**
ela	**com ela**
nós	**connosco** (Pt); **conosco** (Br)
vocês	**com vocês**
eles	**com eles**
elas	**com elas**

Unstressed (clitic) pronouns

The unstressed pronouns combine with verbs and are usually not separated from their verb by any other grammatical structure. When two pronouns (the direct and indirect) are used together, they may combine to form one word. This combination, however, is rarely used in Brazil, where usually only one of the pronouns is used at a time.

Direct and indirect object pronouns

	Indirect	Direct
1st person singular – me	**me**	**me**
2nd person singular – you	**te** (informal) **lhe** (formal)	**te** (informal) **o, a** (formal)
3rd person singular – him, her, it	**lhe**	**o, a** **ele, ela** (Br)
1st person pl – us	**nos**	**nos**
2nd person pl – you	**vos** (informal) (Pt) **lhes** (formal)	**vos** (informal) (Pt) **os, as** (formal) **vocês** (informal) (Br)
3rd person pl – them	**lhes**	**os, as** **eles, elas** (Br)

These forms can combine (although such combinations are rarely heard in Brazil) to form contractions. The contractions are formed by combining the indirect object pronouns *me, te, lhe, nos, vos*, and *lhes* with the third person pronouns *o, a, os, as*. The combinations are:

---

mo, ma, mos, mas
to, ta, tos, tas
lho, lha, lhos, lhas
no-lo, no-la, no-los, no-las
vo-lo, vo-la, vo-los, vo-las
lho, lha, lhos, lhas

Examples:
O Paulo deu as chaves a mim. > O Paulo deu-mas. (Pt)
Paul gave the keys to me. > He gave them to me.

Luísa fez um favor para a Patrícia. > Luísa o fez para a Patrícia. (Br)
Luisa did a favor for Patricia. > Luisa did it for Patricia.

Deram a chave a nós. > No-la deram. (or *Deram-no-la*) (Pt)
They gave the key to us. > They gave it to us.

• Pronoun–verb placement: pronouns preceding the verb

In European and African variants of Portuguese, the clitic usually follows the verb in all cases except the following:

1. after adverbs such as: *ainda, aqui, assim, bastante, bem, já, não, nem, pouco, também, nada, ninguém, nenhum*, etc.
   Examples:
   Ainda não me foi possível ir a Bissau este ano.
   I haven't been able to go to Bissau this year.

2. after interrogative and relative pronouns such as: *como, onde, por que, porque, quando, quanto, que, quem*.
   Examples:
   —Por que não me disseste isso antes?
   Why didn't you tell me that earlier?

   —Porque não me lembrei.
   Because I didn't remember.

3. after *para*
   Example:
   Para te dizer a verdade, estou muito cansado.
   To tell you the truth, I am very tired.

• Pronoun-verb placement: pronouns following the verb

When clitic pronouns follow a verb, they are normally connected with a hyphen.

Example:
Telefona-me. (Pt)
Call me.

In the following cases, however, special forms are required, especially in Portugal and Lusophone Africa.

Infinitives with *o, a, os, as*	The final *–r* of the infinitive is omitted and and an initial *l–* is added to the clitic. The *-a* of the infinitive is written with the *acento agudo* (*á*) and *–e* and *–o* with the circumflex accent (*-ê, -ô*).
	Examples: **Não quero convidá-lo.** I don't want to invite him. **Não quis vê-la.** I didn't want to see her.
Future and conditional forms	The clitic, except in Brazilian Portuguese, may be inserted between the verb root and ending.
	Example: **Ter-te-ia ligado, com certeza.** I would have called you, certainly.
	Also, *veria + a + haver > vê-la-ia* or *haveria de vê-la* (I would see her).
Verb forms ending in *–m* or *–ão*	When combining with these forms, an initial *n–* is added to *o, a, os, as*.
	Examples: **Compraram-nas.** They bought them (to avoid any confusion when pronouncing "conpraram + as" as "conpraram mas," they bought them [for] me).
	Dão-nos aos filhos. They give them to their children (to avoid the hiatus "dão-os").
Verb forms ending in *–s* or *–z*	When combining with these forms, an initial *l–* is added to *o, a, os, as*.
	Example: **Comprámo-lo ontem.** We bought it yesterday.

7.2.3 Reflexive pronouns

The reflexive pronouns are used with reflexive verbs and also if the subject and object of the verb are the same entity. Their placement is the same as that for all other unstressed (clitic) pronouns.

The forms of the reflexive pronouns are the following:

1st person singular – me	**me**
2nd person singular – you	**te** (informal)
	se (formal)
3rd person singular – him, her	**se**
1st person pl – us	**nos**
2nd person pl – you	**se**
3rd person pl – them	**se**

Examples:
Eu penteio-me.
I brush my hair.

Eles se amam muito.
They love each other very much.

The following verbs normally require the reflexive construction:

beneficiar-se (Br)	to reap the benefits from
chamar-se	to be called/named
deitar-se	to go to bed
demorar-se	to take longer
divertir-se	to have fun
lavar-se	to take a bath or shower
levantar-se	to get up
machucar-se (Br)	to hurt oneself (Br)
magoar-se (Pt)	to hurt oneself
olhar-se	to look at oneself in the mirror
pentear-se	to brush one's hair
reunir-se	to get together
sentar-se	to sit down
sentir-se	to feel
vestir-se	to get dressed

The following verbs exist only as reflexive constructions:

apiedar-se de	to feel pity for
condoer-se de	to feel pity for
queixar-se de	to complain about
suicidar-se	to commit suicide

7.2.4 Interrogative pronouns

These are included in Section 10 (Interrogatives).

7.2.5 Relative pronouns

Relative pronouns connect clauses, preventing repetition and redundancy.

The following relative pronouns are invariable and are used as in English:

que (what)
quem (who, whom)
onde (where)

Examples:
O homem que estava na rua, te procurava.
The man that was in the street was looking for you.

Os livros que pediram estão na biblioteca.
The books that they asked for are in the library.

The following relative pronouns agree with the noun that they represent in both gender and number. These are used in more formal registers of Portuguese and in written discourse:

o qual (which) (m)
a qual (which) (f)
cujo (whose) (m)
cuja (whose) (f)

Examples:
Aquelas mulheres, as quais estavam a falar da greve, acabaram por não participar nela. (Pt)
Those women, who (those which) were speaking about the strike, did not participate in the end.

Aquele senhor, cujos filhos estudam com o meu, é meu vizinho.
That man, whose sons study with mine, is my neighbor.

7.2.6 Demonstrative pronouns and adjectives

Demonstrative pronouns and adjectives share the same forms, except that the noun is omitted in the case of the pronouns. They agree in gender and number with the noun that they modify or represent. The plural forms are made by adding a final -s.

Equivalents of "this"/"these":

Masculine	Feminine
este	esta
estes	estas

There are two equivalents of "that"/"those." *Esse* is for objects relatively far from the speaker but near the person addressed, and *aquele* is for objects distant from both.

Masculine	Feminine
esse	essa
esses	essas
aquele	aquela
aqueles	aquelas

There is also a neuter pronoun for each of the above distinctions in distance from the speaker: *isto, isso, aquilo*.

Examples:
Este restaurante é melhor do que aquele ali.
This restaurant is better than that one over there.

Isto é muito importante para vocês.
This is very important for you.

Note: In Brazil, *isso/essa/esse* are often used instead of *isto/esta/este*, without implying greater distance between the object and the speaker.

7.2.7 Indefinite pronouns and adjectives

Indefinite pronouns may function as either a subject or an object. The rules for pluralization, and masculine and feminine forms, are the same as those for nouns, except for *qualquer*, whose gender is invariable and whose plural is *quaisquer*. All negative pronouns are invariable for number.

algum	some
certo	certain
muito	a lot, many, much
nenhum	nothing, none
outro	another, other
pouco	a little, few
tanto	as much, as many
vário	various, several
todo	all

Examples:

Não tenho tanto dinheiro como gostaria.
I don't have as much money as I would like.

Sei de algumas pessoas que falam várias línguas africanas, mas não conheço nenhuma.
I know of some people who can speak several African languages, but I don't know any.

The following pronouns, which generally function as true pronouns (are not followed by any noun), are invariable:

algo	certain, something
alguém	somebody
cada	a little, few
nada	a lot, many, much
ninguém	nobody
outrem	other
tudo	nothing, none

Examples:

O advogado disse que o seu cliente não tinha mais nada a declarar, que já tinha dito tudo o que havia a dizer aos jornalistas.
The lawyer said that his client had no more comments, that he had already said everything to the journalists.

7.2.8 Possessive pronouns and adjectives

The rules for use and formation of the possessive pronouns are explained in Section 4.4.3.

8 Adverbs

Adverbs fall into several categories. Depending on their type, they may either follow or precede the verb that they modify. Adverbs are invariable and do not agree in either gender or number with the subjects of their verbs.

8.1 Adverbs of manner formed from adjectives

Adverbs of manner have adjectives as their roots. They are formed from the feminine singular form of the adjective root and describe the manner in which the action is performed. To the root, the ending *–mente* is added which corresponds to the English "–ly." Adverbs of manner generally follow the verb.

Examples:
falsa (false) – falsamente (falsely)
teimosa (stubborn) – teimosamente (stubbornly)

O golfinho nadou rapidamente com a sua cria.
The dolphin swam rapidly with her calf.

Note: In the case of adjectives whose feminine forms do not end in *–a* (for formation of feminines, see Section 4.1), simply add *–mente*.

Examples:
veloz (quick)-velozmente (quickly)
alegre (happy)-alegremente (happily)

8.2 Adverbs of time, place, quantity, and manner with autonomous forms

These adverbs of time, place, quantity, and manner generally follow the verb they modify. Any adverb which may precede a verb is marked with a dagger ([†]).

8.2.1 Adverbs of time

agora[†]	now
amanhã[†]	tomorrow
anteontem[†]	the day before yesterday
cedo	early
depois[†]	afterwards, after
hoje[†]	today, nowadays
já[†]	already
logo	later, soon
nunca[†]	never
ontem[†]	yesterday
sempre[†]	always (In Brazilian Portuguese, *sempre* usually precedes the verb)
tarde	late

Examples:

Já comi.
I already ate/I have already eaten.

Chegaram ontem.
They arrived yesterday.

Os convidados chegam amanhã no avião das 11.
The guests arrive tomorrow on the 11 o'clock plane.

8.2.2 Adverbs of place

aí[†]	there (next to the person addressed)
ali[†]	there (far from the speaker and addressee)
aqui[†]	here
lá[†], acolá (Pt)	(over) there

Example:
Quando chegarem lá, vão ter uma surpresa.
When you arrive there, you will have a surprise.

8.2.3 Adverbs of manner

assim	so, this way, then
bem	well
depressa	quickly
devagar	slowly
mal	poorly, badly
só, sozinho	alone

Examples:

O pobre homem ficou só depois da morte de sua mulher.
The poor man was alone after the death of his wife.

É importante dirigir devagar na neve.
It is important to drive slowly in the snow.

8.2.4 Adverbs of quantity

bastante	very
demais	too much
demasiado	too much
mais	more
menos	less
muito[†]	very
pouco	little
quase[†]	almost

Examples:

Nadei muito na praia.
I swam a lot at the beach.

Quase caí ao atravessar a rua.
I almost fell crossing the street.

8.3 Adverbs of affirmation and negation

Adverbs of affirmation always precede the verb they modify and the verb may be omitted.

assim assim, mais ou menos	so–so
certamente	certainly, surely
efe(c)tivamente	really, as a matter of fact
realmente	really
sempre	always
sim	yes
também	also

Examples:

Você vem conosco à festa na sexta-feira? Sim!
Are you coming with us to the party on Friday? Yes!

Telefono-te ou passo por aí. (Pt)
I will either call you or stop by.

179

Adverbs of negation also precede the verb that is modified and can also stand alone in spoken discourse.

de forma alguma	under no circumstances
de forma nenhuma/de nenhuma forma	under no circumstances
de modo nenhum/de nenhum modo	under no circumstances
não	no, not
nem	neither, nor
nunca	never
também não	neither

Examples:

Não, nunca iria com você de forma nenhuma!
No, I wouldn't go with you under any circumstances!

Não sei, nem me interessa.
No, I don't know, nor am I interested.

9 Comparatives and superlatives

9.1 Comparatives of inequality

9.1.1 Comparing qualities

In order to form comparatives of inequality in Portuguese, neither the adjectives nor adverbs are modified. Adjectives must always agree with the first item being compared in both number and gender. The following contruction is utilized:

1st item + verb + *mais* (more) or *menos* (less) + adjective or adverb + *do que* + 2nd item

Examples:
Eu sou mais alto do que você.
I am taller than you.

Hoje em dia as pessoas são mais felizes do que antigamente.
Nowadays people are happier than before.
The same construction with *menos do que* is used to express "less than."

Example:
Um rato é menos inteligente do que um chimpanzé.
A rat is less intelligent than a chimpanzee.

Note: The word *do* may be, and often is, omitted in comparative constructions, both in spoken and written discourse.

9.1.2 Comparing quantities

The following construction is used when comparing quantities of nouns:

1st item + verb + *mais* or *menos* + noun + *do que* + 2nd item

In order to form comparatives of inequality, the forms *mais (do) que* and *menos (do) que* are used to denote "more than" or "less than."

Example:
Estudo mais horas do que tu, or **Estudo mais horas que tu.**
I study more hours than you.

Example:
Ele tem mais amigos do que seu irmão.
He has more friends than his brother.

9.1.3 Special comparative (and superlative) adjectives and adverbs

The following adjectives and adverbs are used in place of the structures with *mais* and *menos*:

melhor (better/best)
pior (worse/worst)
menor (smaller/smallest)
maior (bigger/biggest)

Example:
Ayrton Senna era melhor piloto de Fórmula 1 que muitos outros mais conhecidos.
Ayrton Senna was a better Formula 1 driver than many other, better-known ones.

9.2 Comparisons of equality

The English "as–as" construction is expressed with *tão* or *tanto como*.

9.2.1 Quality

In order to convey that two items share the same quality, the following construction is utilized (in the case of comparisons of adjectives, the adjective agrees in number and gender with the first item, while adverbs are invariable):

1st item + verb + *tão* + adjective or adverb + *como* (or *quanto*) + 2nd item

Examples:
O meu carro é tão potente como o do Carlos.
My car is as fast as Carl's.

O Jorge mente tão descaradamente como a Catarina.
George lies as openly as Catherine.

In spoken discourse and informal circumstances, the comparative structure may be reduced to "que nem": **Rogério é teimoso que nem (um) jerico** (Roger is stubborn as a mule).

9.2.2   Quantity

In order to form comparatives of equality, the form *tanto/a/os/as* is used to signify "as much as" or "as many as."

Example:
Não falo tanto como tu.
I don't speak as much as you (do).

The following construction is used when comparing quantities of nouns:

1st item + verb + *tanto/a/os/as* + noun + *do que* + 2nd item

Example:
Isabel tem tantos sapatos como Imelda Marcos.
Isabel has as many shoes as Imelda Marcos.

Note: When modifying nouns, *tanto* is used and its inflected forms agree with the nouns shared by both items.

9.3   Superlatives

The superlative (*grau superlativo*) in Portuguese expresses the idea of maximum superiority or inferiority compared to the other members of a group, or the group in its totality. In English, this is expressed generally with "the most/least + modifier or noun." In Portuguese the corresponding structures are the following:

9.3.1   The superlative with adjectives

Verb + definite article (or definite article + noun) + *mais/menos* + adjective

Examples:
O meu pai é o mais alto da família.
My father is the tallest in the family.

O Pedro e a Flora são os alunos mais aplicados da turma.
Peter and Flora are the most diligent students in the class.

O Pedro é o mais competente.
Peter is the most competent.

Note: While in English the preposition "in" precedes the group of comparison, in Portuguese *de* is used. The group can be omitted, as in English.

9.3.2   The superlative with adverbs and nouns

In Portuguese, an anaphoric or repetitive construction is used to express the superlative with nouns or adverbs. The structure is the following:

subject + *ser* + relative pronoun + verb + *mais/menos* + adverb or noun

Note: in the slot reserved for the relative pronoun, the following items may be inserted:

o/a/os/as + implied noun + *que*
o que, a que, os que, as que
quem

Examples:
Roberto é quem corre mais depressa de toda a equipe.
Robert is the one who runs the fastest in the whole team (Robert runs the fastest).

Pelé é o futebolista que ganhou mais fama no mundo.
Pele is the soccer player who gained the most fame in the world (Pele is the most famous soccer player in the world).

9.3.3   The superlative with verbs

A similar anaphoric structure is used to express the superlative with verbs:

subject + *ser* + relative pronoun + verb + *mais/menos*

With this structure, any adverbial phrases may precede the verb, and with them the adverbs *mais/menos.*

Examples:
Camilo Castelo Branco é o romancista que mais escreveu no século XIX em Portugal.
or
Camilo Castelo Branco é o romancista que escreveu mais no século XIX em Portugal.
Camilo Castelo Branco is the novelist who wrote the most in the nineteenth century in Portugal.

10 Interrogatives

10.1 Yes/no questions

Yes/no questions are expressed with a rise in intonation in Portuguese and do not require any special structure. There is no subject-verb inversion or auxiliary required, as in English.

Example:
Tem tempo para um cafezinho?
Do you have time for a coffee?

10.2 Wh-words or question words

Questions in Portuguese are formed with the question word preceding the verb. Again, there is no subject-verb inversion or auxiliary verb required.

Example:
Quantos anos você tem?
How old are you?

When the verb used takes a preposition, that preposition will be the first word in the phrase.

Example:
A que horas chegaram?
At what time did you arrive?

Interrogative words and phrases

preposition + **que** + noun	to which
como	how
de onde	from where

onde	where
o que	what
para onde	to where
por que	why
Porquê? (Pt)/Por quê? (Br)	Why? (this is used as a sentence in itself)
quando	when
quanto/a	how much
quantos/as	how many
quem	who, whom
qual/quais	which

11 Fields of meaning – vocabulary extension

This section presents vocabulary from a number of semantic fields. The words chosen here are ones in which Portuguese vocabulary presents a large number of synonyms with slightly different uses, as well as vocabulary areas in which English and Portuguese may have either major differences or nuances. The information is presented in list form: the most general Portuguese word at the top of the diagram with progression to the most specific. The material here may be accessed either via the English title of each diagram (arranged alphabetically) or via the individual Portuguese words, all of which are listed in the Portuguese word index at the end of the book.

The symbol + indicates a cover term or most general word which fits most uses.

To agree	**+ estar de acordo** **+ concordar com alguém** **pôr-se de acordo** to agree in general with someone **concordar [em género e número]** to agree (in gender and number, i.e. grammatical agreement) **aceder a fazer alguma coisa** concordar em fazer alguma coisa to agree to do something **consentir em** **aceitar** to accept to do something, to agree to do something (not necessarily by choice)
To annoy	**+ aborrecer** **chatear** (R1) to annoy, to bother **enfadar-se** to become annoyed

	+ **enfadar**
	entediar
	to annoy, to bother
	molestar (R3)
	to annoy, to hurt

Anger

Adjectives	+ **zangado**
	furioso
	furibundo
	enraivecido
	furious, enraged
	estar pior que um urso/pirurso (R1) (Pt)
	to be as mad or grumpy as a bear
Verbs	+ **zangar-se**
	ficar zangado
	to become/be angry
	alterar-se (R3)
	to become annoyed (showing one's anger)
	encolerizar-se
	exasperar (-se)
	irar (-se)
	to become furious or upset

Appearance

Nouns	+ **aparência**
	aspecto
	ar
	general appearance
	semblante (R3)
	cara (Pt)/**rosto** (Br)
	facial appearance
Verbs	+ **aparentar**
	to appear
	parecer
	to seem
	entrar
	aparecer
	comparecer
	mostrar-se
	mostrar a cara
	pôr o nariz de fora (R1)
	to make an appearance

Approval

Adjectives	**fabuloso** fabulous
	estupendo stupendous
	fantástico fantastic
	incrível incredible
	excelente excellent
	admirável admirable
	+ ó(p)timo **tremendo** great
	The following expressions are all R1: **porreiro** (Pt) **legal** (Br) **jóia** (Br) **beleza** (Br) **fixe** (Pt) great or cool in US English
Verbs	**+ aprovar** to approve
	dar "luz verde" (R1) to give the green light / to give the go ahead
	dar "carta branca" (R1) give the OK
	passar (uma proposta/de ano) to pass
	ratificar to ratify
Nouns	**+ aprovação** approval
	autorização authorization
	ratificação ratification

To ask	+ **perguntar** **fazer uma pergunta** to ask a question
	perguntar por alguém to ask for someone
	+ **pedir** **solicitar** (R3) to ask for (something)
	suplicar **rogar** (R3) to beg for
	exigir **demandar** (R3) to demand
	requerer (R3) to require, to request

Back

Nouns	+ **as costas** (of a person, of a chair)
	dorso (of an animal)
	lombada (of a book)
	+ **armazém ou depósito** + **fundos** (Br) (of a store)
Prepositions	+ **atrás** **por detrás** at the back of, behind
	na parte de trás (Pt) in/at the back (of a house, etc.)
Verbs	+ **regressar** **voltar** **estar de volta** to go/come back, to return
	devolver to return something
	apoiar alguém ou uma proposta to back up someone or something
	fazer marcha atrás to back (up) (a car)

	voltar as costas to turn one's back/ to abandon
	telefonar, ligar de volta/ de novo to call back
Ball	**+ bola**
	esfera, globo sphere, globe
	redondinha, esférico (Pt) (R1) soccer ball, (commentator's slang)
	novelo ball (of yarn)
	berlinde (Pt)/**bola de gude** (Br) marble
	divertir-se imenso (Pt)/**curtir à beça** (Br) to have a ball (figurative)
Beautiful	**+ bela** **bonita** **linda** **atraente** **gira** (Pt) (R1) (for women)
	+ belo **atraente** (for men)
	The following are all R1 and can be used for men, women, or things: **jeitoso** **um broto** (Br) **lindinho** (Br) **borrachinho** (Pt) **um pão** (Pt)
	bonitinho **giro** (Pt) **fofinho** (Pt) **fofura**
	um bonequinho/uma bonequinha for children (cute)
	magnífico **belíssimo** **lindíssimo** (of things such as works of art)

To become	+ **transformar-se (em)** + noun
	chegar a ser + noun
	to become something
	fazer-se: presupposes an organic growth or evolution (of an individual night/day)
	Example:
	Ele fez-se um homem maduro muito rápido.
	He became a mature man very quickly.
	tornar-se: emphasizes the process of transformation.
	Example:
	São Paulo tornou-se um estado muito importante no início do século xx.
	São Paulo became a very important state at the beginning of the twentieth century.
	ficar: emphasizes the result of an evolution
	Example:
	Juliana ficou rica do dia para a noite com a herança do seu pai.
	Juliana became rich overnight with her father's inheritance.

To begin, beginning

Nouns	+ **princípio**
	início
	começo
Verbs	+ **começar**
	iniciar
	principiar
	to begin, to start
	travar amizade
	to begin a friendship
	entabular (conversa, relações/ sentimentos)
	to begin a conversation, to begin a sentimental/amorous relationship (R3)
Verb plus infinitive	+ **começar a**
	começar por
	dar início a
	pôr-se a
	to begin + infinitive

Derivatives	**o/a principiante** beginner **mestre de ceremónias (Pt)/cerimônias (Br)** master of ceremonies (who starts an event)
Boat	**+ barco** **barco a remos** row boat **barco a motor** motor boat **barco à vela** sail boat, yacht **barcaça** barge **bote** **lancha** medium sized boat **caravela** small sailing ship (used in early modern Europe) **navio** ship **transatlântico** ocean liner
Bottle	**+ garrafa** **garrafão** five liter (one gallon) bottle **garrafa térmica/termos** thermos flask **jarro** pitcher **cantil** canteen **botija [de água quente]** (Pt) hot water bottle for warming up a bed **frasco** small plastic or glass bottle, flask **biberon/ão** (Pt) baby bottle **engarrafamento** bottleneck (e.g. causing traffic congestion)

Boy/Girl

Boy	+ **bebé** (Pt)/**bebê** (Br)
	nením (Br)
	male baby
	menino (can also be "young man" in Brazil)
	moleque (Br)
	pivete (Pt) (R1)
	miúdo (Pt) (R1)
	kid
	puto (Pt; means "male prostitute" in Br)
	rapaz
	moço (also "man") (regional use in Pt, but not in Br)
	young man
Girl	+ **bebé/bebê**
	nením (Br)
	bebézinha
	female baby
	menina
	child; young woman (Br)
	miúda (Pt)
	female child/kid
	rapariga (Pt; means "prostitute" in Br)
	moça (regional use in Pt, but not in Br)
	young woman

Brake

Nouns	+ **freio** (Br)/**travão** (Pt)
Verbs	+ **frear** (Br)/**travar** (Pt)

Brave

Adjectives	+ **corajoso**
	brave, courageous
	valente
	valiant, brave
	bravo
	brave and easily angered (Br)
	destemido (R3)
	fearless
	intrépido (R3)
	intrepid

	audacioso, audaz **arrojado** audacious, daring
Verbs	**+ ter coragem** **ser corajoso** to be brave
	arriscar (-se) **atrever-se** to dare
	correr riscos to risk, run risks
Expression	*Admirável Mundo Novo* *Brave New World*

To break	**+ partir** **quebrar** (R3 in Pt, R2 in Br)
	fra(c)turar (R3; medical) to fracture
	desfazer **despedaçar** **estilhaçar** **fazer em pedaços** to break into pieces
	dar notícias em primeira mão to break the news (to someone)
	romper/acabar com alguém numa **relação amorosa** to break up with someone
	infringir a lei (R2/R3) to break the law
	romper/desrespeitar/furar (R1) **um** **contrato** to break a contract, agreement

Buttocks/Backside	
Nouns	**+ traseiro** **nádegas** **assento** **rabo** rear, bum **cu** (R1*) **bunda** (Br) (R1*) **bundão** (Br) (R1*) arse, ass

Expressions	**estar pelado/em pelo** to be naked/butt naked/stark (naked)
	rabo de cavalo ponytail
	beata cigarette butt
	cauda tail
	meter o rabo entre as pernas to show fear, admit defeat or give in (literally "to put one's tail between one's legs")
	olhar pelo rabo do olho (R1) to see through the tail of one's eye

Climb

Verbs	**+ subir** to climb (as in stairs, a road, a mountain)
	trepar to climb (including trees)
	fazer escalada to rock climb
Expressions and derivatives	**trepadeira** ivy or any other plant that climbs walls
	trepar pelas paredes to get very angry, to go up the wall

Coarse	**+ basto** **cerrado** **espesso** **rude**
	áspero (for textures)
	grosseiro **incivilizado** **inculto** **não cultivado** **agreste** **não polido** **tosco** (for people)

Call

Nouns	**+ chamamento** call (act of calling)
	+ chamada **ligação** **(o) telefonema** (Pt) **apitadela** (Pt) **ligada** (Br) telephone call
	convocatória (R3) call/invitation to appear before a formally constituted body or panel
	chamada de ordem (R3) call to order
	invocação (R3) call, invocation, apostrophe
Verbs	**+ chamar** to call (e.g. somebody's name)
	chamar-se to call oneself, be named
	ligar **telefonar** (Pt) **chamar** (Br) **apitar** (Pt) to call, phone
	convocar/marcar uma reunião to call a meeting
	chamar à ordem to call to order
	invocar (R3) to invoke
	mandar recolher **recolher, retirar do mercado** to recall (a defective product)

Change

Nouns	**+ mudança** **alteração** (R3) alteration, change
	transformação **evolução** **progressão** (gradual or progressive) change

	troca exchange
	troco change (small money)
Verbs	**+ mudar** to change (in quality); to move (house)
	alterar (R2) to change
	transformar to transform
	trocar **dar em troca** to exchange (for)
	cambiar to change currency
	mudar de vida **emendar-se** to change/improve one's lifestyle
Expression	**um troca-tintas** (Pt) someone who gets things muddled, misattributes quotes, etc.

Coat

Nouns	**+ casaco** **paletó (para homem)** (Br) coat
	(o) blaiser (Pt) coat, blazer
	sobretudo overcoat
	(o) impermeável waterproof coat, mac
	kispo (Pt) **parka** wind breaker
	bata white coat worn by doctor or scientist
	(o) bibe (Pt) coat worn at a private school in lieu of uniform

avental
apron, smock

camada
coating, layer (e.g. paint)

Verbs	**+ passar uma camada** to coat (with paint or similar substance) **impermeabilizar** to waterproof

Competition

Nouns	**+ competição** **concurso** contest, competition **(o/a) concorrente** competitor
Adjectives	**+ competitivo** competitive (person, sport) **concorrido** hotly contested (a lot of people enter for the event) **renhido** close run (match, race)
Verbs	**+ competir** to compete **concorrer** to run (as a candidate); to apply for (a position or grant); to enter (something for a competition) **jogar com/contra** to compete/play against (e.g. another team)

Corner

Nouns	**+ canto** (inside) corner **esquina** outside or street corner **quina** corner of a piece of furniture **recanto** quiet corner (e.g. in city)

Verb	**+ enclausurar** **pôr contra a parede** to corner, get someone with their back to the wall
Expression	**o canto do olho** the corner of the eye

Count

Nouns	**+ (a) contagem** **número** **numeração** **enumeração** count, reckoning, enumeration
Verbs	**+ contar** to count **numerar** **enumerar** to number, enumerate
Expressions	**contar com alguém** to count on someone **Quem conta acrescenta sempre um cónto** A person telling a story always adds something to it

Crime/criminal

Nouns	**+ (o) crime** crime **transgressão da lei** **infra(c)ção** crime (in law), offence **pecado** sin, shame **taxa de criminalidade** crime rate **criminoso** criminal **bandido** bandit **(o/a) fora-da-lei** outlaw

	(o/a) **assaltante** assailant, robber
	o ladrão/a ladra thief
	(o) **escroque** (R1) crook, swindler
Adjectives	+ **criminoso** criminal (action)
	criminal criminal (system, court)
Verbs	+ **cometer um crime** to commit a crime
	estar envolvido num crime to be involved in a crime
	transgredir (R3) **infringir** (tr) **desrespeitar/não respeitar a lei** to break the law
	roubar, assaltar to assault, rob (e.g. person, bank)
	pecar to sin
To cut	+ **cortar** to cut
	partir to split, slice
	amputar to amputate
	podar to prune
	reduzir to cut down (reduce in size or quantity)
	dividir **sec(c)ionar** (R3) to cut into sections
	suprimir **apagar** to cut out, delete

	talhar
	abater
	to cut down (e.g. tree), to carve (*talhar*)
	truncar
	to cut short, truncate

To damage, spoil	+ **estragar**
	to damage
	arruinar
	danificar (R3)
	to ruin
	maltratar
	to damage, mistreat
	desintegrar
	to disintegrate
	deteriorar (R3)
	to deteriorate
	destruir
	to destroy

To deceive

Verbs	+ **enganar**
	to deceive
	pregar uma partida a (R1)
	to play a joke on
	defraudar
	to cheat/swindle
	dissimular (R3)
	to dissimulate
	seduzir
	to seduce
	ser infiel a
	to be unfaithful to, cheat on
Expression	**passar uma rasteira a**
	to trip (somebody) up (figurative)

Defeat, win, beat

Nouns	+ **vitória**
	victory
	+ **derrota**
	defeat

	conquista conquest
	triunfo triumph
	subjugação subjugation
Verbs	**+ vencer** **+ derrotar** (R2, R3) to vanquish, defeat
	conquistar to conquer, overcome
	triunfar sobre to triumph over (somebody, something)
	subjugar (R3) to subjugate, overcome, conquer
	+ ganhar to earn, win
	ganhar a uma pessoa num desporto **(Pt)/esporte** (Br) to beat someone at a sport
	bater to beat (someone in a game)
Expression	**bater alguém aos pontos** to beat somebody by many points, beat them hands down

Destroy, destruction

Nouns	**+ destruição** destruction
	demolição demolition
	desmantelamento (R3) dismantling
	(o) derrube (R3 in Pt) knock–down
	desperdício **desbarato** wasting, laying waste
	despovoamento **assolamento** devastation

inutilização
(act of) rendering something useless

estragação
(act of) laying waste

destroços
(smashed) pieces, fragments

esmagamento
(act of) squashing, crushing

trituração
breaking into pieces

máquina britadora
britadeira
crusher

brita
gravel

aniquilamento
annihilation

ruina
ruin

Verbs	**+ destruir** **desfazer** to destroy

demolir
to demolish, pull down

desmantelar
to dismantle, take down

derrubar
deitar abaixo (R1)
to knock down, tear down

desbaratar
to waste

despovoar
devastar
to devastate, depopulate, lay waste

assolar (R3)
to raze

desfazer
inutilizar
estragar
to spoil, smash, render useless

destroçar
to smash to pieces (also used figuratively
for strong emotions, heartbreak, "wrecking"
by grief)

esmagar
to smash, squash, crush

triturar
to break into pieces

britar
to crush, shatter, break up (asphalt or cement)

calcar
to stamp on (and destroy)

aniquilar
to annihilate

arruinar
to ruin

Dirty

Nouns	+ **sujidade** (Pt)/**sujeira** (Br) **porcaria** (R1) (general noun applied to conditions of physical and moral filth)
	(a) imundice (R3) filth, foulness
	pocilga (R1) pigsty
	porco pig (also adj: filthy, disgusting) (R1)
Adjectives	+ **sujo** dirty
	insalubre (R3) insalubrious
	manchado stained
	imundo (R3) filthy
	lamacento muddy
	poeirento dusty
	tiznado grimy; sun-tanned

impuro
impure

imoral
immoral

obsceno
obscene

em más condições de higiene
unhygienic

asqueroso
disgusting, revolting

merdento (R1)
disgusting

sórdido
sordid, filthy

pecaminhoso
(said of a situation conducive to
sinfulness; shameful)

Dispute

Nouns	**+ discussão** **contenda** (R3) **disputa** **altercação** (R3) **querela** (R3) dispute, argument **+ debate** **polêmica** (Br)/**polémica** (Pt) debate **desafio** challenge **luta** **peleja** (R3) (physical) fight **briga** (Br) **bulha** (Pt) (R1) **bate-boca** (Br) (R1) **berros** (R1) noisy dispute
Expressions	**chegar a vias de facto** (Pt) (R1) **andar aos murros** (Pt) to come to blows **meter a mão na cara** (Br) to hit someone generally in the face

To dive	**+ mergulhar** **lançar-se** to dive
	deitar-se a (água/mar/rio/lago) to dive (from a height into the water/sea/river/lake)
	submergir-se to submerge, to go down
	fazer/praticar mergulho to practice high-diving
	fazer mergulho to scuba dive
	lançar-se a **abalançar-se a** to dive (into something) (a project, etc.)
	precipitar-se to rush or hasten (into something)
Drawing, sketch, *design*	**+ desenho** **esboço** drawing, sketch
	contorno **silhueta** outline
	traçado layout (of streets, etc.)
	(o) diagrama **(o) esquema** diagram
Edge	**+ beira** **+ bordo**
	orla (of water, bank, shore)
	(o) limite limit
	(a) margem margin of a page
	aresta (of a cube)
	fio **bico** **ponta** sharp edge or point of a knife, etc.

207

	canto (of coin, book)
To enjoy oneself	
Verbs	**+ divertir-se** **entreter-se** **distrair-se** **gozar** (Pt)
	disfrutar to enjoy (something)
	gozar (Br) (R1*) to have sexual pleasure
Expression	**bon vivant** (French borrowing)
Evildoer	**+ malfeitor** **malvado/a** wicked person
	criminoso/a **delinquente** criminal
	arruaceiro hooligan
	canalha **sem-vergonha** swine
	pícaro (used to be R1, now R3) rogue
	malandro streetwise (Br), wicked (Pt)
	velhaco rascal, scoundrel
To examine	**+examinar**
	inspe(c)cionar to inspect
	perscrutar (R3) **esquadrinhar** (R3)
	fazer o escrutínio to court the votes

indagar (R3)
investigar
pesquisar
to investigate

apalpar o terreno (R1)
to test the waters

Face

Nouns	+ cara (Pt) (used in all senses of "face" including figurative; also "heads" when tossing coin) + rosto (Br) + semblante (R3) a face (R3) aspecto + superfície surface, face (e.g. of the earth)
Verbs	+ estar em frente de estar defronte de (R3) to be in front of dar para to face, overlook (a street etc.) olhar para encarar to face (a person) enfrentar to look at, face up to (a person) fazer frente a to stand up to confrontar to confront voltar a cara para olhar para encarar to move or turn to face dar a outra face to give the other side

Fat (of people)

+ gordo/a

corpulento/a
robusto/a
thick, strong

		obeso/a (R3) obese
		rechonchudo/a (R1) **gordalhufo/a** (R1) **gordito/a** (R1) **gordinho/a** (R1) plump, chubby
		fofo/a (Br) tubby
		pançudo (R1) **a pança** (R1) (of belly)
To find		+ **encontrar** **achar**
		descobrir to discover, to find out
		dar com **tropeçar** em **topar com** (R1) **dar de caras com** (Pt) to find unexpectedly, to run into
		notar to notice
		reconhecer to recognize
		revelar to reveal, find out, reveal to others
Fire		
Nouns		+ **fogo**
		incêndio fire (which destroys property, such as a house fire or forest fire)
		lume cooking, fire, light (for a cigarette)
		fogo (Br) cooking fire
		fogueira camp fire
Verbs		**acender o fogo** to light the fire

pôr fogo a
to set something on fire

pegar fogo (intr)
to catch fire

Fortune, luck, chance	+ **sorte** fortune
	má sorte **azar** bad luck
	(boa) sorte good luck
	acaso **por acaso** **por casualidade** by chance
	destino **sina** (R3) **fado** (R3) destiny
	ventura chance

Full

Adjectives	+ **cheio**
	completo full to capacity (e.g. hotel, parking lot)
	repleto full to capacity (volume)
	cheio full up
	cheio a abarrotar crammed full
	+ **farto** over-full, stuffed
	atestado (Pt) full to the brim (e.g. gas tank)
	transbordante **a transbordar** overflowing
	entupido clogged up

	inchado swollen
	empanturrado **empazinado** full fed
	pleno full (in the abstract, e.g. "em plena vista" = in full view)
Verb	**+ encher** **rechear** to fill up, stuff up
Noun	**recheio** filling (cake, pillow); stuffing (turkey)

Funny

Adjectives	**+ engraçado** **divertido** amusing
	cômico (Br)/**cómico** (Pt) comical
	com piada **com graça** (Pt) **espirituoso** (Pt) (R3) witty
	hilariante hilarious
	estranho funny (peculiar)
	surprendente surprising
	esquisito odd
Expression	**rir a bandeiras despregadas** (Pt) to laugh very loudly (lit. "with widespread flags")

Gift

Nouns	**+ presente** **oferta** **dádiva** (R3) **oferta**

doação
donativo
donation

oferenda (R3)
offering (in a church)

talento
dote (f)
talent, natural gift

Verbs	+ dar

atribuir
to attribute

entregar
to deliver, to hand in, to hand over

proporcionar (R3)
to provide (support, a living)

abastecer
fornecer
to supply (with food, water)

oferecer
doar
brindar (alguém com)
to donate, to offer (somebody something)

dotar
dar um dote
to endow, to give a dowry

conceder
otorgar (R3)
to grant, to bestow (prize, honor, award)

louvar
elogiar
to give praise

ceder
render-se
to give in, to give up

repartir
distribuir
to give out, to distribute

destinar (R3)
to earmark something to be given (to somebody)

ser dotado
to be gifted

Expression	**dar a alma ao Criador** to die (lit. "give one's soul to the Creator")
Glass	+ **vidro** glass (the substance)
	+ **(o) cristal** pane of glass, covering of glass (watch), type of glass, crystal
	+ **copo** drinking glass (for any liquid [Pt], for water [Br])
	xícara (Br) coffee cup
	chávena (Pt) coffee or tea cup (Pt) tea cup (Br)
	taça (Br) tea cup
	caneca (Pt) mug
	óculos eye glasses, spectacles
	binóculos binoculars
	monóculo monocle
	lupa magnifying glass
	+ **janela** glass in window, windowpane
To grab, to get hold of	+ **pegar** + **agarrar** **tomar**
	colher **recolher** to pick up, to gather
	agarrar-se a to grip, to hold on to
	apoderar-se de to seize, to take control of
	+ **apanhar** to catch

Group of people	**+ grupo**
	associação
	agrupamento
	reunião
	formal group of people (gathered for a specific purpose); meeting
	+ conjunto
	(general)
	+ equipa (Pt)
	equipe (Br)
	time (Br)
	team
	partido
	political party
	fa(c)ção
	faction
	banda
	bank, music-making group
To grow (tr)	**+ criar**
	to raise children or animals
	cultivar
	to raise/grow crops or plants
To grow (intr)	**+ crescer**
	aumentar
	incrementar
	to increase in quantity
	ampliar
	expandir
	extender
	to expand, to extend
	alargar
	prolongar
	to increase in length (including time)
	elevar-se
	to increase in height
	desenvolver-se
	to develop
	engrandecer
	to inflate, to praise (usually to an unjustifiable degree)
	ficar importante
	to grow in importance

Gun	+ **arma** (de fogo) firearm
	revólver revolver
	pistola pistol
	espingarda **(o) fuzil** **(o) rifle** (Br) rifle
	escopeta shotgun
	canhão cannon
	artilheria artillery
Hair	+ **cabelo** hair on the human head
	+ **pêlo** hair on body
	barba beard
	bigode mustache
	pera goatee
	pêlo fur, coat of an animal
	cãs grey hairs
	peluche hair (of stuffed toy)
	crina mane of a horse
	juba lion's mane
To happen, to take *place, to occur*	+ **acontecer** + **ocorrer** (R2) + **passar-se** + **suceder**

	ter lugar **celebrar-se** (for events)
	realizar-se to happen (in fulfillment of an expectation or preparation)
	sobrevir (R3) to happen unexpectedly
Happy	**+ feliz** **+ contente** **satisfeito** happy (*feliz* is used with either *ser* or *estar*, *contente* and *satisfeito* with *estar* only)
	alegre cheerful
	jovial (R2–R3) jovial
	ditoso (R3) fortunate
Heel	**+ (o) calcanhar** (of foot)
	tacão of shoe
	salto (alto) high heel
To help	**+ ajudar**
	auxiliar (R2) **socorrer** (R2) to aid (suggests danger or problems)
	dar uma mão (R1) **dar uma ajuda** to give a hand
	+ apoiar to support
	+ assistir to assist (R2)
	facilitar to facilitate, to make easier

Hill	**+ (o) monte** large hill
	morro **cerro** **colina** **montículo** (R3) small hill
	encosta slope (on a road)
	(o) declive short, steep slope
	ladeira hillside
	penhasco **penha** rocky hill or cliff
	ribanceiro **despenhadeiro** embankment, cliff
To hit	**+ bater (em)** to beat
	dar porrada (R1) **dar pancada em** (R1) to beat up
	dar um murro to strike a blow (on)
	golpear to strike, punch, strike with a knife
	dar uma bofetada to give (somebody) a slap on the face
	chicotear to lash/whip
	pegar-se com to get in a fight with (also "to get involved")
	chocar com to crash into (of e.g. car)
	acertar em to hit (a target)
	bater um tambor to hit/beat a drum
	ir para cama to hit the sack

Hole	**+ abertura** opening
	+ buraco hole in the ground (or in any surface)
	cavidade (R2–R3) cavity (in the ground)
	poço well
	furo puncture
	orifício orifice
	fenda **brecha** gap (in a fence)
	toca rabbit hole
	cárie cavity in a tooth
	cova small hole, depression
	depressão (R3) depression
Holidays	**+ férias** holiday, vacation
	+ festas **dia festivo** **festividade** religious holiday
	feriado **dia feriado** public holiday
	folga soldier's leave; day off (for person working day shifts)
To hurry	**+ (estar com/ter) pressa** to be in a hurry
	apressar-se **andar com pressa** to move/act in a hurry
	diligenciar (R3) to hasten, to order something done in a hurry

Improvement	**melhoramento** (Br) (R2–R3) (general)
	melhoria (R2–R3) (of economy or performance)
	melhora (of health)
	avanços advances
	+ **progresso** progress
To inform	+ **informar** **inteirar** (R3)
	avisar **notificar** to notify
	anunciar to announce
	indicar **comunicar** to communicate
	advertir **acautelar** **prevenir** to warn
Intelligent	+ **inteligente** intelligent
	esperto (R1) sharp, shrewd, smart
	astuto **perspicaz** (R2–R3) **sagaz** (R2–R3) astute, perspicacious
	penetrante sharp
	lúcido **clarividente** clear-sighted
	genial brilliant
	vivo quick-minded

Journey	+ (a) viagem
	jornada (R2–R3) day trip
	périplo (R3) sea voyage around all or part of coastline; the narrative of such a voyage
	excursão excursion, guided group tour
	volta short journey (e.g. round the block)
	traje(c)to trajectory
Kind, nice	+ **amável**
	amistoso **amigável** friendly
	benévolo **benigno** **benevolente** (R3) gentle
	carinhoso **afe(c)tuoso** affectionate
	+ **bom** **bondoso** **bonacheirão** (R1) good-natured (a good person)
	bem-intencionado well-meaning
To know	+ **saber** to have knowledge of, to have information memorized, to know how to do something
	+ **conhecer** to be familiar with, to know people, to be acquainted with, to have been to a place
Language	+ **língua**
	(o) idioma (R2) language (French, Portuguese, etc.)
	(a) linguagem style or register of language

	fala spoken language **jargão, gíria** (Pt) jargon, professional specialized terminology (Pt) **calão** (Pt), **gíria** (Br) slang
Lazy, idle	+ **preguiçoso** **indolente** (R2–R3) **ocioso** (R3) relatively lazy or with free time **gandulo** (R1) (Pt), **vagabundo** (Br) a lazy person, good for nothing
Leader, boss	+ **chefe** leader, boss, chief **caudilho** political leader **(o) cacique** local boss, local tyrant **(o) cabecilha** leader of a marginal group **patrão** boss, business owner **(o/a) gerente** manager, boss **(o/a) responsável** person in charge **dono** (R1) **senhor** **proprietário** owner, master
To leave (tr)	+ **deixar** + **deixar de** (+ inf) to quit (doing something) **abandonar** to stop doing something, to quit a project, course of study etc.
To leave (intr)	+ **sair** **partir** (used with destinations)

zarpar
(of a ship [R3]; of persons [R1])

ir-se
ir-se embora
to leave a place, to go away

apartar-se de (R3)
afastar-se de (R2)
to wander from

embarcar
to leave (as on a boat), embark

Money	+ **dinheiro**
	(o) capital capital
	moeda coin; (foreign) currency
	massa (R1) (Pt); **grana** (Br) cash
	troco change
	fortuna **dinherão** (R1) fortune, a great deal of money

Name	
Nouns	+ **(o) nome** first/Christian name (Br); name (in general) (Pt)
	nome de ba(p)tismo first/Christian name (Pt)
	apelido surname (Pt); nickname (Br)
	sobrenome surname (Br)
	alcunha nickname (Pt)
Verbs	+ **pôr/dar um nome** to name
	nomear (R2–R3) to appoint, name, invoke a name

Native

Nouns	+ **nativo** (also adj)
	+ **natural de** person born in . . .
	indígena **autóctone** (R3) **aborigem** (R2–R3) person born in (a place); of/from (a particular place; also applies to objects, cultures, etc.; also adj)
Adjectives	**oriundo** (R3) coming from a place, but not necessarily born there
	natal (denotes origin from a particular place: city, town, country etc.)
	materna **nativa** **primeira** native (of language)

Old

Old	+ **velho**
	ancião **mais velho** (of people)
	+ **antigo** ancient; former
	vetusto (R3) ancient
	arcaico old, archaic
	antiquado old fashioned
	gasto (for old clothes)

Outskirts (of a city)	+ **arredores** district, any area outside of a city; suburbs
	periferia lit. outside circumference of a city; used for its surroundings in general

	subúrbios cidade-satélite cidade-dormitório suburb, satellite/dormitory town
Pattern	+ modelo model
	+ exemplo example, sample
	mostra, amostra sample
	+ forma form
	desenho design, drawing
	padrão pattern (fabric, surface)
Pay	+ salário ordenado wages, salary
	pagamento payment
	honorário (Pt), pro labore (Br) professional fee
	jorna soldo (for soldiers) day's pay
	mensalidade monthly fee
	anualidade annual fee
	subsídio de férias (Pt) the extra check paid in Portugal in August
Pool, Pond	+ lago lake
	charco small pond
	poça large puddle
	+ piscina swimming pool

Poor	+ **pobre** **necessitado** **indigente** (R3) **desvalido** (R2–R3) **remediado** short of money, needy **pobre** **desgraçado** **desamparado** unfortunate **desprotegido** unprotected **mau** (Pt) **em mau estado** **ruim** (Br) in a poor state, poor quality, ruinous
To take *possession of*	+ **apoderar-se de** **deitar mão a** (R1) to take possession/control of (in general) + **tirar/pegar** (Br) to take away **apropriar-se de** (R2–R3) **assenhorar-se de** (R3) to appropriate **usurpar** (R2–R3) **roubar** to usurp, steal, take away from
Poster, notice	+ **letreiro** sign **póster** **cartaz** poster **anúncio** advertisement **aviso, placa** warning sign or notice
Proud	+ **orgulhoso (de)** proud (of) (may be positive or negative; takes *estar*)

arrogante
soberbo (R3)
altivo (R2)
altaneiro (used to be R1, now R3)
arrogant, haughty, stuck up

presunçoso
presumptuous

vaidoso
vain

convencido (Pt) (R1)
metido (Br) (R1)
presumido
boastful

To put	+ **pôr**
	colocar **posar** **deitar** **posicionar** (R2–R3) **situar** (R2–R3) to place, to situate
	meter **introduzir** (R2–R3) to insert, to put in(side)
	postar-se to post (e.g. a police officer); to station
	encostar to put against
To raise	+ **levantar** **elevar** (R2) **erguer** (R2–R3) to pick up, to elevate
	subir to put up (such as blinds, a window) to rise (prices) (intr)
To rebel	+ **rebelar-se**
	insurre(c)cionar-se (R2–R3) **revoltar-se** **insurgir-se** (R2–R3) to revolt
	ser indisciplinado, insubordinado to be insubordinate

	questionar to question (e.g. authority)
	amotinar-se to riot, to mutiny
Rich	**+ rico**
	ricaço (R1) **endinheirado** very rich
	abastado well off
	novo-rico nouveau riche
	pesado, com muita gordura rich (of food)
To ride	**andar a cavalo** **cavalgar** to ride a horse
	andar de bicicleta to ride a bicycle
	+ andar de **viajar em** to ride a car, bus, train etc.
Ring	**aro** ring or hoop
	círculo circle
	argola hoop, ring of metal
	anel finger ring
	anel de noivado engagement ring
	aliança wedding band / ring
	selo signet ring
	chaveiro key ring
	brinco earring
	argola (for curtains, gymnastics)

Rock, stone	**+ pedra** rock (in geological sense, a medium sized rock or stone which one might lift)
	rocha **rochedo** large rock or boulder
	penha boulder
	pedrinha pebble
	macadame brita gravel
Room	**+ sala**
	quarto bedroom; hotel room (Pt)
	apartamento (Br) hotel room
	sala de estar living room
	salão salon
	aposento (R3) room used for formal occasions
	quarto/sala de banho (Pt) **banheiro** (Br) bathroom
	sala de jantar dining room
	assoalhadas (Pt), **quartos** (Br) (Pt) used for rooms in a house, as when counting their total number
	escritório personal office
	(o) gabinete personal office (Pt); office shared by a number of persons (Br)
	sítio (Pt) **(o) lugar** **(o) local** (empty) space, site
	espaço space (in general)

Sad	+ **triste**
	pouco contente
	descontente
	discontented
	pessimista
	tristonho (R1)
	sad, gloomy
	melancólico
	melancholy
	desconsolado
	inconsolable
	aflito
	worried, anxious
	+ **infeliz**
	unhappy
	abatido
	deprimido
	depressed, dejected
	lamentável
	lamentable (of actions)
	desafortunado (R3)
	desditoso (R3)
	unfortunate
To say, to speak, to talk	+ **falar** (intr)
	to speak (intr), to speak a language, to say
	+ **dizer**
	+ **falar** (tr)
	to say, to tell (Br)
	conversar
	bater um papo (R1) (Br)
	to chat, to converse
	expressar-se
	to express
	pronunciar
	to pronounce
	fofocar (Br)
	to gossip
	mexericar (Pt), **lançar boatos**
	to speak badly about someone, to spread rumours

To see	+ ver
	+ olhar para to look at
	observar examinar to observe, examine, look at closely
	notar to notice, take notice
	descobrir perceber dar conta (de) que to notice, to realize
	presenciar testemunhar to witness
	sondar to scan, survey
	distinguir to distinguish
	fitar olhar fixamente seguir com os olhos to stare at
	dar uma vista de olhos (Pt) dar uma olhada (Br) dar uma olhadela (Pt) to take a quick look
To send	+ mandar (R1–R2) + enviar (R2)
	despachar to dispatch
	pôr no correio to send by mail
	expedir (R2–R3) to expedite
	remeter (R2) to remit
To shine	+ brilhar luzir reluzir to shine (literally)
	resplandecer to shine, to blaze

	rutilar (R3) **cintilar** to sparkle
	refulgir (R3) to glitter (diamonds)
	incandecer to shine so brightly that it blinds, to flash brightly
	fulgurar (R3) to shine brightly
	piscar to flash intermittently
	bruxulear (R3) **tremeluzir** to flicker (candle)
	faiscar to twinkle
	+ brilhar **sobressair** to stand out, to shine (figurative)
To shoot	**+ disparar** **atirar** to fire a weapon
	ferir to wound
	matar to kill
	matar de um tiro to shoot dead
	atirar em **dar um tiro em** to shoot at
	atirar **lançar** **arremessar** (R2–R3) to throw a ball
	xutar (a bola) **dar um pontapé/xuto** to shoot (kick a ball)
Shop, store	**+ loja**
	armazém department store

negócio
comércio
business

mercado
market (open-air or covered)

feira
open-air market (of a periodic nature)

centro comercial
shopping
mall, shopping center

minimercado
small grocery store

supermercado
supermarket

hipermercado
superstore

To show	+ **mostar**
	indicar (R2) **salientar** (R2) **pôr em evidência** to point out
	apontar para to point to
	demonstrar to demonstrate
	aparecer to show up
	revelar **desvendar** to reveal, to unveil
Side	+ **lado**
	perfil **lado** (of a person)
	de lado on the side
	flanco (of animal), flank
	ladeira **vertente** **lado** (of hill)

	lado (of record, audio cassette)
	alcatra side of meat
	borda **beira** **margem** edge
	orla shore, bank
To steal, to rob	+ **roubar** **furtar** (R3) **subtrair** (R3) **fanar** (R1) **limpar** **surripiar** (R1)
	desviar to embezzle
	assaltar to hold up, mug (rob somebody on the street)
Stick	+ **pau** stick of wood (in general); stick, handle to hold something with (e.g. of broom, lollipop)
	vara pole
	bastão (R3) **bengala** cane
	varinha stick, wand
	galhos sticks for kindling
Storm	+ **tempestade** storm (in general)
	+ **trovoada** thunderstorm
	(o) temporal **tormenta** (R3) strong storm

borrasca (R3)
storm with rain and wind, sometimes at sea

nevão
snowstorm

tempestade de granizo
hailstorm

String

Nouns	**+ corda** rope **cordel** **guita** thin rope, twine **cordão** cord **fio** thread **linha** fishing line, sewing thread **filamento** filament (metal ore, bodily tissue, light bulb) **atacador** (Pt), **cordão** (Br) (Pt) shoelace
Expressions	**estar por um fio** to be hanging by a thread **romance de cordel** (Br) a short, melodramatic, popular story sold at a fair or by a peddler (like an old English chapbook); so called because they were displayed on a string for sale **mexer os/ums cordéis/cordelinos** to pull some strings (exercise influence)
Strong (of people)	**+ forte** **com força** **musculoso** muscular **robusto** solid, tough **sólido** hefty

	vigoroso **enérgico** vigorous
	poderoso powerful
	valente strong in character
Stubborn	**teimoso**
	obstinado (R2) **persistente** **porfiado** (R3) persistent
	tenaz (R2–R3) **pertinaz** (R2–R3) **contumaz** (R3) tenacious, stubborn
	cabeçudo (Pt) (R1) **cabeça dura** (R1) pig-headed, hard-headed
Stupid	+ **estúpido**
	parvo (Pt) (R1) dumb
	tonto foolish, silly, stupid
	idiota imbecile **cretino** idiot(ic)
	burro (R1) **atrasado mental** (R1) idiot, fool
	estúpido que nem uma porta dumb as a doorknob
To take	+ **levar** to carry, to take, to take away
	+ **tomar** to take medicine, notes; also to drink, to have breakfast
	conduzir (Pt) **guiar** (Pt) **dirigir** (Br) to drive

	guiar to lead
	transportar to transport
	tirar to take a picture or photocopy
Teacher	+ **professor**
	senhor(a) professor(a) **setor/setora (senhor[a] doubtor[a]) (Pt)** high school teacher
	docente university instructor, lecturer
	catedrático (Pt), titular (Br) university (full) professor
	mestre teacher to an apprentice; also a person with a master's degree
Thin (of people)	+ **magro** **delgado** (R2–R3)
	esbelto slim, svelte (usually positive, whereas *magro* is not)
	enxuto lean (has positive connotation)
	ossudo bony
	descarnado **cadavérico** thin (in the face), cadaverous
	esquelético skeletal
	famélico (R2–R3) skinny, starving
	definhado emaciated
	espantalho (R1) a scarecrow
	um pau de virar tripas (Pt) skinny as a rail
To think	+ **pensar**
	+ **pensar que** to think that

+ **achar que**
to think/believe that

imaginar que
to imagine that

ser de opinião que
opinar que (R3)
to be of the opinion that

conceber
to conceive

inventar
to invent, to think up

refle(c)tir sobre (R2)
to reflect upon

ficar a pensar em
to brood over

ponderar sobre
to ponder

meditar em/sobre
to meditate on

pensar de
to think about (in questions)

Example:
O que pensa das notícias?
What do you think of the news?

pensar em
to think about

Example:
Não penso muito em política.
I do not think much about politics.

Tooth	+ **dente** (m)
	dentes de leite first teeth, milk teeth
	molar molar
	canino canine tooth
	incisivos front teeth
	dente do siso wisdom tooth

Top	+ (a) parte de cima (a) parte superior top (general) + topo (o) alto (de) (adjective used as noun) top, high part (of e.g. stairs) pico cimo (of hill or mountain) copa (of tree) topo (of table; of list) (a) superfície (of liquid) teto top of bus; ceiling telhado roof
Trick	+ truque + engano act of deception treta (R1) lie travessura act of mischief (o) ardil (R2–R3) (o) estratagema ruse burla artimanha tramóia hoax, dirty trick pregar uma partida a (Pt) to play a trick on

To try	
with verbs	+ tentar fazer alguma coisa procurar fazer alguma coisa (R2) to try to do something esforçar-se por fazer alguma coisa to make the effort to do something

	esmerar-se por fazer alguma coisa (R2–R3) to try one's hardest to do something
with nouns	+ **tentar alguma coisa** to attempt something
	provar alguma coisa to try, to taste something
	ensaiar alguma coisa to test out something
	experimentar to try on (clothing)
	fazer uma experiência to experiment (scientific), put to the test
Wall	+ **parede** interior wall of building
	muro exterior wall (not part of a building)
	taipa wall of garden, small outside wall
	muralha large wall of city, castle
	barreira barrier
To waste	+ **desperdiçar**
	+ **perder** (time, opportunity)
	desbaratar **deitar dinheiro à rua** (R1) **atirar dinheiro pela janela** (R1) to waste money
	atirar fora to throw away
To wear	+ **usar** + **levar** + **pôr** (to put on) **vestir** **trazer posto/vestido** to wear
	estrear to wear for the first time
	+ **gastar** to wear out

Wind	+ **vento**
	rajada gust of wind
	brisa breeze
	(o) vendaval gale
	(o) furacão hurricane
	torvelinho **remoinho** whirlwind
Window	+ **janela** window in house or building
	clarabóia skylight
	vidro windowpane, glass
	vitral stained-glass window
	guiché cashier's window
	o pára-brisas windshield (car)
Work	+ **trabalho**
	emprego **posto** **ocupação** post, position, job
	tarefa **(o) labor** (R3) task
	tacho (R1) paid post
	obra a work, a work of art, public works
	trabalho de casa **tarefa de casa** (Br) **dever de casa** homework

12 Portuguese for Spanish speakers

Portuguese has many similarities with the Spanish language. Especially in its written form, Portuguese may be read by an educated Spanish speaker. However, there are some important differences which can mislead the Spanish speaker who is either a student of Portuguese, a translator, or traveling in a Portuguese-speaking country. This section is designed in order to help Spanish speakers best utilize their own language skills to master, or at least function in, Portuguese.

12.1 Pronunciation

Pronunciation is one of the chief areas in which Portuguese (with all its many variants) and Spanish differ. The following equivalents and differences are noted in order to help avoid confusion. Many sounds are similar or identical in Spanish and Portuguese; knowing when to distinguish between these and those that are different greatly aids communication. This is not a phonetic prescription for pronunciation, but a guide to help Spanish speakers with comprehension of spoken Portuguese.

The following letters are pronounced the same (or almost the same) in Spanish and Portuguese:

b	<u>b</u>onito	pretty
c	<u>c</u>asa	house
d	<u>d</u>á	he/she gives
	d is always pronounced the same in Portuguese, whether at the beginning or between vowels, unlike in Spanish.	
f	con<u>f</u>iar	to trust
h (silent)	<u>h</u>otel	

i	**I̲sabel**	
m	**m̲otor**	
n	**n̲ada**	nothing
p	**p̲obre**	poor

Note: The initial *p* in *psicologia* etc. is not silent in Portuguese.

qu	**q̲ue**	what/that

Note: *Qu* is pronounced the same as Spanish *cu* before *a* or *o*. *Quando* is therefore pronounced the same as Spanish *cuando.*

t	**t̲er**	to have

Note: In most areas of central and southern Brazil, the letter *t* before *i* and unstressed *e* is pronounced like *ch* in Spanish.

u	**p̲eru**	turkey

The following letters are pronounced differently from those in Spanish, at least in some positions.

a	*a* is pronounced the same in both languages when stressed: cá [a]. In European Portuguese, the unstressed *a* is pronounced [α], similar to the schwa sound in "butter" in English.
ç	The *ç* is pronounced the same as the Spanish *s*.
d	*Note:* In some areas of Brazil (such as Rio de Janeiro), the letter *d* before *i* and unstressed *e* is pronounced as the "*j*" in English.
e	*e* is pronounced approximately the same in both languages when stressed. In European Portuguese, the final *e* when unstressed is pronounced similar to English schwa, as in the English unstressed "a." In Brazilian Portuguese, the final unstressed *e* is pronounced the same as the Portuguese *i*.

243

For accented letters, *é* [ɛ] is pronounced similar to the Spanish *e* in *estar* while *ê* [e] is pronounced similar to the sound in *queso*.

g	*g* [g] is pronounced the same as Spanish before *a*, *o*, and *u*, as in Spanish *gato*. However, it is pronounced similarly to the Argentine pronounciation of 'y' [ʒ] as in *yo* before an *e* or *i*.
j	*j* is always pronounced like the *g* before *e* and *i* (see above).
l	In European Portuguese, the initial *l* is more palatalized (similar to the Catalan *l*) – *lata*. In Brazil, an *l* at the end of a syllable or word is pronounced like *u* – *Bra<u>sil</u>* [ziw].
o	In Portuguese, the final -*o* is pronounced the same as *u*. Otherwise, while there are nuances (degree of openness: *o avô*, *a avó*), the Portuguese *o* is similar to that in Spanish.
r	The single *r* within words is pronounced the same as the Spanish tap *r*- *caro*. When a word ends in *r*, the pronunciation varies widely in different regions in Brazil, Portugal, and Lusophone Africa.
rr	The standard pronunciation for initial *r* and *rr* is similar to that of the Spanish *j*.
s	Single *s* is pronounced as in Spanish at the beginning of words – *Sara*. The single *s* is pronounced like the English *z* between vowels – *casa*. The single *s* is usually pronounced rather like the English "sh" at the end of words such as *elefantes* in Portugal, Rio de Janeiro, and in standard Portuguese in Lusophone Africa.
ss	Double *ss* is pronounced like the *s* in Spanish.
v	The letter *v* is pronounced like the English *v* – *volume*.

x	The letter *x* can have different pronunciations. It is often pronounced approximately like the English *sh*, in particular at the beginning of a word – *México*, *xadrez*, *xarope* – or before *t* and *p* – *sexta*. It can also be pronounced *z* – *existir* – or as [ks], as in *sexo*.
z	In most positions, *z* is pronounced like the English letter. The letter *z* is pronounced like the [ʒ] in "pleasure" at the end of a word – *capaz*.

In Portuguese, all vowels can be nasalized and this process is shown in writing by the tilde "~", or an 'm' or 'n' after the vowel.

Examples:
um (one)
pão (bread)
conceito (concept)

12.2   Cognates with different genders

Some words have different genders in Portuguese and Spanish. The following are important ones to remember:

Portuguese	Spanish	English
a análise	*el/la análisis*	analysis
a arte	*el arte*	art
a árvore	*el árbol*	tree
a fraude	*el fraude*	fraud
a lineagem	*el linaje*	lineage
a ordem	*el/la orden*	order
a percentagem	*el porcentaje*	percentage
a viagem	*el viaje*	trip
o cárcere	*la cárcel*	jail
o computador	*la computadora*	computer
o dote	*la dote*	dowry
o leite	*la leche*	milk
o mar	*el/la mar*	sea
o massacre	*la masacre*	massacre
o mel	*la miel*	honey
o morango	*la fresa*	strawberry
o paradoxo	*la paradoja*	paradox
o postal	*la postal*	postcard

o sal	*la sal*	salt
o sangue	*la sangre*	blood
o sinal	*la señal*	sign

Also, all letters of the alphabet are masculine in Portuguese while they are feminine in Spanish: *o 'a'* (the letter 'a')

12.3   False cognates

Many Portuguese words look similar or identical to Spanish words, especially if they share a common (usually Latin) source. These words are called cognates. However, there are many misleading or false cognates.

The following words are false cognates in Spanish and Portuguese.

Portuguese	English equivalent	Spanish	English equivalent
achar	to find, to believe	*hallar*	to find
apenas	only	*apenas*	barely
aula (f)	class	*el aula*	classroom
bastante	much, a lot	*bastante*	enough
Braga	the city Braga	*braga*	panties
cadeira (f)	chair	*la cadera*	hip
calção (m)	shorts	*el calzón*	underwear (Latin America)
contestar	to contest	*contestar*	to answer
costas (f, pl)	the back	*la costa*	coast
embaraçada	embarrassed	*embarazada*	pregnant
esquisito	weird	*exquisito*	exquisite
fraco	weak	*flaco*	thin
frente (f)	the front	*la frente*	forehead
gente (f)	we	*la gente*	people
graça (f)	humor/grace	*la grasa*	grease/fat
lista (f)	the list	*la lista*	list; ready (f)
noivo/a	betrothed/fiancé(e)	*novio/a*	boyfriend/girlfriend
obrigado/a	thank you	*obligado/a*	forced
película (f)	plastic film, but movie is *filme*	*la película*	any film
pelo (m)	body hair	*el pelo*	hair
(estar) pronto	to be ready	*pronto*	fast
precioso	valuable	*precioso*	lovely, beautiful
raro	rare	*raro*	strange
roxo	purple	*rojo*	red
sugestão (f)	suggestion	*sugestión*	a fantasy

tapa (m) (Br)	a tap (hit)	*la tapa*	snack (Spain); lid or bottle cap (Latin America)
tão pouco	so little	*tampoco*	neither
todavia	however	*todavía*	still
todo	all of	*todo*	everything

12.4 Spelling

The following equivalents can be observed for Portuguese/Spanish cognates:

1. words ending in *–ción* and *–sión* end in *–ção* or *–são* in Portuguese.
    Examples:
    televisión – **televisão**
    concepción – **concepção** (Pt), **conceção** (Br)

2. The ending *–ería* in Spanish has as its equivalent *–aria* in Portuguese.
    Example:
    zapatería – **sapataria**

3. The word *y* ("and") in Spanish is always spelled *e* in Portuguese.

4. The letters *ll* and *j* in Spanish have several equivalents in Portuguese.
    Examples:
    viejo – **velho**
    llevar – **levar**
    amarillo – **amarelo**
    Sevilla – **Sevilha**

5. The letter *ñ* in Spanish is often represented by the combination *nh* (but still pronounced 'ny') in Portuguese.
    Examples:
    cañon – **canhão**
    España – **Espanha**

12.5 *Ser* with location

Ser is used with any permanent location in Portuguese (where Spanish would use *estar*).

Example:
San Francisco está en California – **São Francisco é na Califórnia.**
San Francisco is in California.

12.6   Differences in verb tense and mode

1. Most verb tenses and modes are used similarly in Portuguese and in
    Spanish, most notably the past tenses of the indicative. For compound
    tenses, the auxiliary verb in Portuguese is *ter*, while in Spanish it is
    haber.

    Examples:
    Quando era criança, passava sempre as férias na praia.
    Cuando era niño, siempre pasaba mis vacaciones en la playa.
    When I was a child, I always used to spend my vacation on the beach.

    No sábado passado não comi feijoada.
    El sábado pasado no comí "feijoada."
    Last Saturday, I didn't eat bean stew.

    **Quando ele soube das promoções, já tinha comprado os
    sapatos, que foram bem caros.**
    *Cuando supo de los saldos, ya había comprado los zapatos, que fueron muy
    caros.*
    When he heard about the sales, he had already bought the shoes,
    which were very expensive.

    For further information about the Portuguese tenses, please refer to
    Sections 5.1.2, 5.1.3 and 5.2.2.

2. Spanish does not have a future subjunctive (Section 5.3.3) or a personal
    infinitive (Section 5.1.5). It normally uses the present indicative or
    present subjunctive where Portuguese uses the future subjunctive, and
    an ordinary infinitive, or a subjunctive construction, where Portuguese
    uses the personal infinitive.

    Examples:
    **Se vocês quiserem ir em Santa Catarina durante o
    fim-de-semana, me liguem. (Br)**
    Se ustedes quieren ir a Santa Catarina este fin de semana, llámenme.
    If you want to go to Santa Catarina during the weekend, call me.

    **Tu precisas de lhes emprestar a tua máquina fotográfica para
    eles poderem tirar boas fotos.**
    Tienes que prestarles tu cámara para que puedan sacar buenas fotos.
    You have to lend them your camera so that they can take good
    pictures.

3. With concessive-type clauses (i.e. those introduced by "although," etc.), Portuguese uses only the subjunctive mode (except for a few occurrences with *a pesar de que*, mainly in Brazilian Portuguese), but in Spanish the indicative is regularly used with *aunque* to convey the meaning 'although' as opposed to 'even if':

Examples:

Ainda que seja tarde, tenho de ir ao hospital porque me chamaram.
Aunque es tarde, tengo que ir al hospital porque me han llamado.
Although it is late, I have to go to the hospital because they beeped me.

Aunque sea tarde, tengo que ir al hospital porque me han llamado.
Even if it is late, I [still] have to go to the hospital because they beeped me.

4. Although the use of the present indicative is almost identical in Spanish and in Portuguese, European Portuguese has a periphrastic progressive form (Section 5.8.2), preferring it to the gerund form, whereas in Brazil the gerund is used, as it is in Spanish and English.

Examples:

Estou a escrever uma carta. (Pt)/Estou escrevendo uma carta. (Br)
Estoy escribiendo una carta.
I'm writing a letter.

5. The present perfect in Portuguese signals an event or action that started in the past but continues into the present with some frequency. It is not used to denote a past action in a recent past time-frame, as it is in Peninsular Spanish.

Examples:

Tenho corrido na praia, ultimamente.
He corrido por la playa recientemente.
I've been running on the beach, lately.

Já entreguei o filme ao André.
Ya he entregado la película a Andrés. (Spain)
Ya entregué la película a Andrés. (Latin America)
I've already returned the movie to Andrew/ I already returned the film to Andrew.

For further information on the present perfect in Portuguese, please see Section 5.2.1.

Index of Portuguese words